What
Happy
Women
Know

What
Happy
Women
Know

How New Findings in Positive Psychology Can Change Women's Lives for the Better

Dan Baker, PhD,

Founding director of the Life Enhancement Program at Canyon Ranch
and author of *What Happy People Know*,

and Cathy Greenberg, PhD,

with Ina Yalof

RODALE

© 2007 by Dan Baker, PhD, Cathy Greenberg, PhD, and Ina Yalof

Rodale books may be purchased for business or promotional use or for special sales.
For information, please write to:
Special Markets Department, Rodale Inc., 733 Third Avenue, New York, NY 10017

Printed in the United States of America
Rodale Inc. makes every effort to use acid-free ♾, recycled paper ♻.

Book design by Tara Long

Library of Congress Cataloging-in-Publication Data

Baker, Dan
    What happy women know : how new findings in positive psychology can change women's
lives for the better / Dan Baker and Cathy Greenberg with Ina Yalof.
        p.   cm.
    Includes bibliographical references and index.
    ISBN-13 978-1-59486-545-9   hardcover
    ISBN-10 1-59486-545-0   hardcover
    1. Women—Psychology.   2. Happiness.   I. Greenberg, Cathy.   II. Yalof, Ina L.
III. Title.
HQ1206.B213 2007
155.3'33—dc22   2007010439

Distributed to the trade by Holtzbrinck Publishers

2   4   6   8   10   9   7   5   3   1   hardcover

We inspire and enable people to improve their lives and the world around them

For more of our products visit **rodalestore.com** or call 800-848-4735

For all the women I have counseled over the years:
You have taught me more than you will ever know.

Contents

Acknowledgments

In the process of creating this book, many people have contributed their time and effort in assisting us. We are particularly grateful to our super-agent Richard Pine for his unfailing support and encouragement and for bringing together the principles of this book.

We also are indebted to our sagacious editor, Nancy Hancock, for her energy and enthusiasm throughout the course of this undertaking. Her guidance, dedication, and care has been greatly appreciated.

We were so fortunate to find Benjamin N. Taylor among the 4,000 or so students at Dartmouth College. Ben took time from his studies and his position as executive editor of the Dartmouth College newspaper, to type the transcripts of every interview. Lisa Considine was in on the formative stages of the book and her astute advice at that time proved invaluable. Leslie Garfield also read early drafts of various sections and provided beneficial feedback. Laura Kirtly was always on hand to make our lives easier.

Thanks to Mel and Enid Zuckerman, cofounders of Canyon Ranch, and Jerry Cohen, Canyon Ranch CEO, for providing generous support as well as the perfect environment during our research and writing.

Of all of those who helped us, however, we are most deeply grateful to the several dozen women who shared their lives and their stories with us so that we might share them with our readers. Not every story appears herein—there simply wasn't room—but each of these women contributed a significant piece of the book's foundation. Thank you to all.

Introduction

We all live with the objective of being happy; our lives
are all different and yet the same.

Anne Frank

How happy are you right now? *Do you even know?*

Most women know what makes their partners, children, or friends happy, but when it comes to recognizing what lights up their own lives, they often come up short. If you're looking for happiness, you have to start with the relationship you have with yourself. Is it healthy, loving, and nurturing? Or do you defer to your nay-saying inner critic, as so many women are prone to do?

The world is full of women who are living lives defined by negatives—defined, that is, by what they believe they cannot do and what they do not have. Over the course of my years in practice, too many women have told me they keep looking for happiness, looking for what they want while quietly believing it will never be theirs. *Why even dream?* they ask.

Why not? I answer.

Why not dream about a joyous life? Why not overcome the self-constructed barrier between what your life is and what you want it to be?

Happy women know that they can have meaningful,
fulfilling, and happy lives regardless of life's circumstances.

Come with me and learn what happy women already know.

You can do it.

Starting now.

∴

What Happy Women Know is filled with the stories of women who have led happy lives in spite of life's tribulations or because those circumstances led them on paths they would not otherwise have taken. These are not necessarily the strongest or even the bravest women. Rather, they are people like you and me. What sets them apart is that they were able to integrate their experiences into the narrative of their lives and move on. You will also read stories of women who have always been happy—women who know how to take a *good* life and make it even *better*.

This book follows *What Happy People Know*, which I wrote 5 years ago with Cameron Stauth. When I approached my publisher with the idea of a new book exclusively for and about women, she asked me what was different. What about happiness might be specific to the female gender?

The answer is: far more than even I had imagined. It turns out that much of happiness is gender specific. Let's start with the brain.

As the scientific opportunities to examine the brain grow with each generation of imaging machines, we are able to probe deeper and deeper into its recesses. New research shows that the notion of a unisex brain is no longer viable; in fact, there are vast differences between the male and female brain, but whether these differences are based on genetics, hormones, or a combination of the two is not yet known. What *is* known is that after only 8 weeks in utero, the female brain diverges from the male brain and goes on its merry way.

The neurons in the female brain make more connections in areas that govern communication and emotion, while the neurons of the male brain are more concentrated in the areas that govern sex and aggression, according to the book *The Female Brain*, by Louann Brizendine, MD, a physician and founder of the University of California, San Francisco, Women's and Teens' Mood and Hormone Clinic. This is why women are so much more relationship centered than men are. Dr. Brizendine also cites the following facts:

- Women have 11 percent more neurons for language and hearing than men do (which may be why men never answer when we call them).
- The prefrontal cortex, which is responsible for self-control, is larger and matures earlier in women, which is why women tend to be more patient than men.
- The space allotted to the sex drive in a woman's brain is 2½ times smaller than in a man's brain.
- The hippocampus, which is responsible for emotional memory, is larger and more active in women, which is why they remember emotional events in greater detail.
- The amygdala, which is responsible for aggression, is smaller in women, and therefore they are less likely to take physical risks.

In terms of emotions—which so often impact on happiness—there are many scientifically documented differences between men and women. And, as with the brain, this number is growing all the time. We know, for example, that women appear to vacillate between happiness and sadness far more quickly than men. For instance, when it comes to raising children, women say that it is both more difficult and more rewarding than they could have ever imagined. Women experience more of all emotions except anger, and while they experience two to four times more depression than men, they also report more positive emotion more frequently and more intensely.

Evolution plays a tremendous role in the way happiness reflects on the genders, and you will read a great deal here about the way who we were continues to influence who we are. Back in the Neolithic Age (Stone Age) when humans were evolving, in order for men to function as hunters, they had to be stronger and more aggressive and to think in more strategic terms. Their level of success determined their status and power within their group. It wasn't really all that different from today. Women's primary role was to bear children—an undertaking that then, as now, required support, nurturance, communication, cooperation, and strong relationships. Without these basic standards, there could be no success. What each of the sexes valued and what it was they were valued for most likely set the stage for what they found to be fulfilling and meaningful. Clearly, from the days when their brains were just in the formative stages of human thought and emotion, women and men were on different paths to happiness.

Because what constitutes happiness for men and women differs to such a degree, it also follows that what they think will make them happy must differ as well. To the degree that men spend much more time and energy in the pursuit of power, status, and things, women focus more on relationships, cooperation, and better communication. While men are far more caught up in *having enough*, women are far more engaged in *being enough* and often struggle mightily when they fear they are not.

What Happy Women Know is intended to help you understand the importance of positive emotions and to make it easier for you to find your own happy place. It is also meant to point out how easy it is to fall into the many traps that hinder women in their quest for happiness.

A "happiness trap" is something that appears to offer the key to happiness but does just the opposite: It promises happiness but doesn't deliver. In fact, it often becomes *more* of a trap because when happiness doesn't ensue, people respond by redoubling their efforts. If one cosmetic surgery doesn't do the trick, then surely another one or two or three will.

Six of the most common traps that lead to unhappiness in women comprise the core of this book. These traps could just as easily be called the "if onlys." *If only* I were thinner, *if only* I had more money, *if only* I could meet the man of my dreams, *if only* I could get that next promotion, life would be perfect. No, it wouldn't. Because as happy women already know, these are not the things that deliver the joy in life you are seeking. If you believe they are, happiness will always remain just outside your reach.

Most of the traps you'll find here are based on misplaced fear. Fear comes in many guises and expresses itself in many ways. For women particularly, fear is the product of not being enough. As you will see again and again throughout this book, most women feel as if they are somehow inadequate. If they're remarkably beautiful, they find a feature to hate. If they're incredibly accomplished, they believe they're impostors and that given time, someone will "find them out." Who is ever satisfied? Who ever feels secure? No one. That's because, as will soon become clear, we still have a survival brain that is hardwired to keep us thinking that way.

Woven throughout the chapters is a series of tools—instructions or prescriptions that offer ways to avoid falling into a trap or ways to pull yourself out if you find yourself in one. There are single tools for some of the traps and multiple options for others. Not every tool fits every person, so as you work your way through this mosaic, select the ones you believe will work best for you.

Working the tools requires consciousness, courage, and commitment—all mechanisms that make you responsible to yourself. As with any other skill, the more you practice using these tools, the stronger the neurological connections in your brain will become, and the less you'll have to think about when to put them to work. When the situation arises, you just will.

When rain starts falling, you don't think much about what you need to do; you just get the umbrella and open it. It's that same concept of *habituation*—which we will talk more about later—that will allow you to best incorporate these tools into your daily life.

This book is divided into 10 chapters. The first examines the still-emerging discipline of positive psychology and sets the foundation for what follows. Positive psychology is changing the nature of psychotherapy as we've always known it by developing ways to identify and nurture people's strengths rather than dwelling on what's wrong in their lives. This has been the thrust of my practice at Canyon Ranch in Tucson for the past 20 years—long before the new discipline even had a name.

The next six chapters are given over to discussion of the happiness traps, the first of which is perfectionism. This trap is based on the fear of *not being good enough*. Women who fall into it believe that happiness correlates with a specific goal, such as being thinner, smarter, younger, more beautiful, and more popular. In short: perfect. But perfection is an unattainable illusion. *You can't get there from here!* Women seek perfection because, as you'll learn later, they are biologically wired to do so. This chapter also explores why women invariably choose to compare themselves to someone with an attribute that's higher or better than what they themselves have. Why isn't good enough ever good enough?

Chapter 3 investigates the power of wanton wanting. This trap, based on the fear of not having enough, evolves from thinking that material things will bring bliss. The enticement of happiness works best when we believe that the joy will continue indefinitely, hence the belief that acquiring the new car, the new house, the new spouse will be the solution. The truth is: No, it won't—and lottery winners prove it. Scientific studies show that a few years after hitting the jackpot, lottery winners rate their overall life satisfaction no higher than it was before they won the big bucks.

The next chapter shines a light on women who think they can make themselves happy simply by pleasing everyone else. Unlike her male counterpart's, much of a woman's life is relationship driven, so it comes as no surprise that doing for others can be highly seductive. But when you give a slice of yourself here and a small portion there, a little energy here and a little time there, at some point, you find that there's nothing left for you. And if you're not there for yourself, who will be there for you? This chapter looks at the rationale behind "the disease to please" and suggests the best prescriptions for cure.

Revenge is the name of the game many women erroneously sign up for, and it's the topic of Chapter 5. Who hasn't at one time thought: *I would be so happy if only I could make him jealous, make him love me again, make him dead!* What people don't seem to realize is that if you hold a grudge, you're not only creating a trap for yourself, you're giving yourself a double whammy—first from the inciting event, which has already happened and is presumably over, and then from the fallout, which can last a lifetime. Or not. That's up to you. If you think forgiving him is letting him off the hook, you are mistaken. It's really letting *you* off the hook.

Next is the "I'm nothing without him" trap. One of the ways we entrap ourselves is by wrapping up all our hopes, identity, and sense of destiny in another person (although there are also those whose identities are tied to their possessions or careers). What happens when that person exits our lives? For one thing, the void leaves us with lots of room to grow.

An inability to separate life and career sets the stage for the final trap. Many women invest all their energy in their jobs because work tends to temper our survival fears of not having enough and not being enough. The question is: If you put all your eggs in the work basket, where does that leave you in life? If you think the title of Mme. President and a killer expense account are going to keep you warm at night or ask you sweetly to tie their shoelaces when they come undone, think again. Happiness comes from a full life, and that's contained in one word: *diversification.*

The remaining chapters focus on loss, health and happiness, and the qualities of happy women. The subject of loss may seem misplaced in a book about happiness, but in fact just the opposite is true. Over the course of our lifetimes, we will all lose someone we love, someone we will grieve for. This chapter suggests ways to transcend grief by celebrating life—giving it meaning and purpose and making count those precious moments you spent with the person for whom you now grieve. In the chapter on happiness and health, I leave the subjects of nutrition and exercise to the experts and instead, with the help of some of my colleagues, investigate the roles of sexuality, positive emotion, and the immeasurable importance of connecting with others—all equally fundamental underpinnings of a woman's happiness.

The final chapter offers a series of vignettes illustrating the qualities of happy women. These are first-person accounts of 18 women who we believe personify what's right in the world. Many of these women have been through traumatic experiences and have emerged both positive and healthier on the other side. Their experiences have much to teach us all.

We found our subjects in all corners of the United States. As a benefit of my position at Canyon Ranch, I have been in contact with some of the most interesting women in this country; women who flourish, who thrive, who are incredible human beings. Over time, a number of them have stood out in my mind, and when I contemplated putting together this book on happy women, I started making a list. I asked myself, *Who is a happy woman, and why?* I came up with a number of names for different reasons. But when I looked at them across the board, there also were commonalities. For instance, the vast majority of these women were proactive. They didn't wait for life to come to them—they went out and engaged in it. They participated in the creation of their destinies.

Not all the women we interviewed were from my practice at the ranch. Some were friends of friends of friends. My coauthors and I sent carefully drafted e-mails to people we knew, requesting the names of happy and resilient women with interesting stories to tell. We received an overwhelming flood of replies—many from strangers far removed. Such is the power of the Internet. These women couldn't wait to tell their stories. We couldn't wait to hear them.

The women who appear in Chapter 10 (and occasionally elsewhere in the book) are identified by their full names. A short biography of each is appended at the end of that chapter. The women whose case studies are cited throughout the other chapters to illuminate specific points are identified by only their first names, and even these—as well as other distinguishing characteristics and situations—have been altered sufficiently to protect the women's identities.

What Happy Women Know is intended to provide a blueprint to help you find happiness in your life without having to win the lottery or marry Mr. Right or whittle yourself down to a perfect size 2. In fact, I hope you are already a happy woman and that you're reading this book to broaden your blissful horizons. But if you're not; if you're seeking a life that's a whole lot better, or even just "this much" better, then know that happiness is already near.

It's waiting for you.

CHAPTER ONE

Positive Psychology and the Science of Happiness

The US Constitution doesn't guarantee happiness,
only the pursuit of it. You have to catch up with it yourself.

Benjamin Franklin

I'm not sure how long he had been standing there. I was on the telephone when I sensed someone moving about outside my office. He must have heard me hang up, because he appeared within seconds—a tall, fiftyish man with close-cropped gray hair. When I asked if I might help him, he replied, "God, I hope so."

"We just arrived this afternoon," he said. "I'm hoping you'll have time to talk to my wife." I indicated a chair, and he introduced himself as James.

"We've been to a million doctors," he said. "I hear you work miracles."

"I'm hardly a miracle worker," I said, flattered nonetheless. "Suppose you tell me what this is all about."

In the next 10 minutes, he told the story of his wife, Serena, in such a straightforward manner that I wondered how many times he had recited it

1

before. Her parents died when she was 8, and when no relatives could take her in, she landed in foster care. "I'm sure there are many good foster homes," he said, "but Serena wasn't that lucky. Hers was the kind you read about in those tabloids at the supermarket." He then proceeded to paint a detailed—and horrifying—picture of her young life, as she was bounced from foster home to foster home. In the last home, he said, she had been subjected to both sexual and emotional abuse and locked for hours at a time in a darkened closet. Ultimately, she simply ticked off the days until she felt she could survive on her own in the outside world.

At 16, she packed up her meager belongings, walked out the door, and never looked back. James met her when she was working the counter in a tiny takeout shop where he bought his morning coffee. Eventually, they married and adopted two beautiful babies who were now in their early teens. "She has never been able to forget her past, though," he said. "And lately, things seem to be spiraling downward. I'm really worried about her."

We arranged for her to come to my office the next afternoon.

Serena* was a small woman in her midthirties, with shoulder-length dark hair and dull gray eyes. I'll never forget the first thing she said or the sadness in her voice as she said it: "I don't like living like this, Dr. Baker. I've never been happy, and I don't believe I'll ever be happy."

I knew she didn't mean the last part because after all, she was in my office. At least she hadn't given up all hope.

I wanted to tell her that she was wrong, that she could be happy, that happiness is just a way of looking at life. It was clear from the story her

*Names and identifying characteristics of all women described in case studies have been changed to protect their privacy.

husband had recounted that she had courage; she certainly had love, and I believed that if she looked deeply enough, she would find a way to fulfillment as well.

"I don't deserve my family," she said softly.

"And why is that?"

"Because I'm always sad. I put a damper on everything."

Listening to her was like listening to a tape on a player with failing batteries. The word *apathy* came immediately to my mind. Apathy is one of the hallmarks of depression. Given the choice of which I'd rather work with, an apathetic person or an angry one, I'll take the angry person every time. Give me someone who slams a fist on the desk or throws things at the walls over someone who believes there is no hope. Anger is just another negative emotion that eventually gets resolved. Apathy can take far longer. "Why not start at the beginning?" I said.

First she shared some memories of her parents and her early, happy times with them. (At least I knew there was a time when she had experienced true happiness, even if it was nearly three decades ago.) Then she told me how they died in an automobile accident, and she was sent to live with a foster family—the first of many. "The last was the worst," she said. She lowered her gaze to her lap, clasped her hands, and slowly began to speak of the unspeakable. Five minutes into her story, I stopped her in midsentence. "Serena," I said, "tell me about your children."

Immediately, her whole demeanor changed. She told of her son, "an incredible soccer player, captain of his traveling team," and her daughter, who had just starred in a ballet recital and is a marvelous student. As she spoke, her energy perked up, and she even managed a semblance of a smile.

I wasn't surprised. When I meet someone whose world has been rocked, I let them start talking, then I interrupt and ask them to tell me about someone they love or something in their lives they have great appreciation

3

for. In that moment, the brain switches away from the painful subject to process the new topic. And so, almost within a snap of the fingers, Serena shifted from "I'm not good enough. I'm all alone. God help me; what's going to happen to me?" to "I've got these two amazing and beautiful children."

I kept going. "How did they get great?" I asked. "And isn't it remarkable that you can help human beings grow into the kind of people your children are?" I wanted her to recognize that she was a great success at parenting, and I wanted her to tell me so she would hear it herself. Sometimes people can point out the good in everyone else, but when you ask them about the good in themselves, they haven't got a clue.

The conversation drifted back to her past, and again I interrupted her. This time I suggested we take a walk outside.

It was a crystal clear, perfect Tucson day—the kind of day that every guest at Canyon Ranch prays they'll wake up to. As we walked, I said to her, "Serena, I want you to go to the first thing you see that's beautiful."

She stopped at a purple flower that sat on the edge of a still pond. "Look deep into the flower," I said.

She did.

"Now smell it."

She did.

"Now touch it."

She did that, too. Then she looked up at me as if waiting for her next instruction. Instead, I asked her a question, "How do you feel this second?"

"I feel . . . okay."

"Good. Let's go find something else that's beautiful, and you can tell me all about it."

She indicated a tall, beautifully symmetrical cactus, and we repeated the exercise. She said it reminded her of a favorite sculpture, and when I asked how she felt, she just smiled. I think she instinctively knew what was happening.

Here's the thing about love and appreciation. They are both positive emotions, and when you engage in either of them, or any other positive emotions, you cannot simultaneously be miserable. That's because the brain is not wired to process both a positive and a negative at the same time. Two things are important to know about positive and negative emotions. The first is that negative emotions have their place, which is to work for us in acute and sometimes life-threatening situations. Serena was no longer experiencing an acute situation, it's true, but she continued to function as if she were. That's because the human brain habituates to certain circumstances, particularly threatening circumstances that evoke strong negative emotions.

Because she had been down for so long, her neurological pathways had "grooved" so that even if she was no longer in an unpleasant situation, her brain thought she was. Essentially, it was easy for her to perceive threat almost continually. When one is in a state of constant vigilance, it depletes energy, and this was in large part responsible for her flat affect. Try being on guard duty 24/7, and see how you feel.

The second thing that's important to know about human emotions is that the brain's pathways for evocation of negative and positive emotions are different. In other words, you cannot be on two different streets at the same time. What I was doing in Serena's case was helping her to engage the lesser-used pathways of her brain so that eventually she might have a more positive perspective on life.

A Walk in the Desert

Serena's homework for the week she was at the ranch was to take an "appreciation walk" six times a day. Each afternoon, when she returned to my office, I asked her to talk about the beauty she saw around her. After a few days, we moved on to the beauty she saw in her husband, in her children, and finally in herself.

Had I asked her on the first day to talk about the beauty she saw in herself, she would have been stumped because she saw nothing but ugliness. Women and children who are abused by a more physically powerful male often escape the only way they can—by "running away" in their heads. The problem is, they generally can never run quite far enough to completely get away. Compounding that situation is the fact that they see themselves as damaged goods, so they rarely return to who they were prior to the attack. It's a little bit like Dorothy in Oz, who couldn't get home until she accepted herself for who she really was. Serena tried to make some sense of her life by assuming there was something wrong with her, which there wasn't. It was her brain recalling the earlier times. It had never let go because, as you'll see later, it couldn't.

But *she* could.

Today's Serena—the one I had only just met—was a 36-year-old woman who had power and strength and potential she didn't know she had. When I got her to focus on love and beauty, she began to realize there were possibilities out there for her. She had only to look for them.

Once the pump was primed, she could talk about what was good in her life. I believe if we had jumped back into the darkness, we would have exacerbated that darkness. If I had taken her back to the days of the abuse, it would have proved nothing and might have made matters worse. My approach—that is, the approach of positive psychology—does not ignore the pain of life but instead shows how one can exercise the power of choice while engaging life from moment to moment. It is being proactive to a situation rather than reactive. It's one thing to try to fix a tangible object that is broken, but I have never seen the human psyche in that way. The psyche is not something to be repaired in the same way an orthopedist would set a shattered arm.

At our last meeting before she left the ranch, Serena and I discussed what she would do when she got home. She said she wanted to do something to make the world around her a better place. For her children in particular and perhaps, she said, for others as well. "Maybe for foster children. Girls, maybe. Like me." Serena understood that she couldn't erase what had happened to her—it would always be there—but she could transcend it. The memory would remain, but she found a way to live with it constructively and not try to distance herself from it. Essentially, we not only changed the playing field, but we also changed the rules. And it didn't take years of psychotherapy.

The day they left the ranch, Serena and James stopped in to say goodbye. Her eyes were bright, and her husband's eyes reflected hers. She had a new direction now: a purpose and a goal. The apathy was behind her. She saw possibilities in her life. She had hope.

Now, you may be wondering what exactly I did.

The Birth of Positive Psychology

The method I practice is called positive psychology. It is a rapidly growing movement that offers an alternative to clinical psychology. Unlike clinical psychology, which focuses on what's *wrong* with people, positive psychology shifts the emphasis to finding what's *right* with them. It works on the premise that identifying a person's virtues, strengths, and character and then building on them is far more helpful than pointing out a person's weaknesses and trying to fix them.

If asked to characterize positive psychology in general, I would say it is *the study of the good life*. It's the study of what's working. It's essential to understand that positive psychology is not only for the troubled. To the contrary. The idea is to take a life, even a good and happy life, and make it more meaningful. Even the happiest of people can and do benefit from this new discipline.

As you may have noticed with Serena, my method doesn't include burying life's painful experiences. I don't think anyone could, even if they wanted to. Rather, it embraces them as learning experiences and suggests using the new wisdom in a positive, practical way. Serena had a horrific childhood. For years, she visited doctors who tried to help her but failed because they kept asking her to relive the worst of what she'd been through. When I saw her, I quickly let her know I was more interested in her life now than in her past. I encouraged her to appreciate what she currently had, with an eye toward helping her find the possibilities in her future. Positive psychology is all about looking for possibilities.

Could Freud Have Been Wrong?

The science of clinical psychology began in Europe in 1879 as a discipline that concerned itself with things that impair the human mind, such as depression, neurosis, paranoia, anxiety, and delusions. Several decades later, Sigmund Freud introduced his theory of the unconscious and how it influences human behavior. He believed that people who kept their traumatic experiences locked away in a "black box" of memory, which he later dubbed the subconscious, would never be able to fully enjoy their lives until those deep-seated memories were brought to light—that is, to consciousness. Through *psychoanalysis*—the term he used for his new method of working with patients—Dr. Freud was convinced that he could talk a patient back to the experiences of childhood. Exploring what occurred during that time would be immeasurably beneficial for bringing them peace—or so he thought.

Dr. Freud's work laid the foundation for clinical psychology in America, where for years it was considered a subset of psychiatry. In 1920, Alfred Adler, MD, convened a meeting of his psychologist peers and suggested the profession would be more highly regarded if it fashioned itself after Western medical practices. Doctors were directed to diagnose and relieve patients' symptoms, and those patients who could function in society were considered "cured."

Based on a scale that ranges from minus five to plus five—minus five being illness and plus five being a flourishing good life—the goal of clinical psychologists was to bring patients from a state of illness to a neutral state, or from minus five to zero. There was no interest in going beyond that to anything that might make people feel fulfilled, engaged, or meaningfully happy. It was tantamount to the chairman of Standard Oil getting up in front of the major stockholders and telling them, "Our goal this year is to break even."

How long would that guy have a job?

An editor I know told me that she worked for a publishing house where one of the measurements used to evaluate job performance included a system for tracking how many books she and her coworkers turned over to production. "If you were supposed to edit 10 books a year, then you started at minus 10. When you turned in a couple of books, the report showed you at a minus 8, and so on. The idea was, you worked your way toward the goal—zero. Boy, was that depressing."

Prevention is an improvement, but it is still founded in allopathic (disease-fighting, not health-enhancing) medicine. The basic premise of prevention is that you should do something good for yourself or something bad may happen. But positive psychology's focus is on living the good life, so the premise is to do something good for yourself and something good may happen. The thrilling thing about positive psychology is that it looks to develop one's potential as far as possible.

A Dog's Life

The seeds of the new discipline were sown in 1964 when Martin Seligman, PhD, then a 21-year-old University of Pennsylvania graduate student in psychology, collaborated on an experiment that would ultimately define his life's work. In an animal behavior laboratory, Dr. Seligman and the other researchers placed a number of dogs in wire cages and subjected them to a series of random small electric shocks from which they could not escape. After repeated unsuccessful attempts to get away, the dogs eventually just laid there, whimpering and accepting their fate.

A short time later, the same dogs were moved to similar cages, but this time only half of each cage was electrified. This time, when they received the shocks, they could easily make a small leap to safety on the other side of the cage. Yet when the electricity was turned on, only some of the dogs tried to escape it. Others remained as they had been, passively enduring the discomfort. It was as if those dogs had learned to be helpless.

Dr. Seligman went on to successfully apply this concept of learned helplessness as a model for certain types of depression in people. He theorized that some people who feel beset by problems have a similarly learned mindset—they've stopped believing they can do anything to improve their situation.

For decades, as he worked on the theory of learned helplessness, Dr. Seligman kept wondering about the other group of dogs—the ones who leaped to safety. That curiosity led him onto a whole new path, this time looking at high levels of adaptivity in humans. What is it, he wondered, that imparts psychological strength in some people and not others? Why do some people learn helplessness—I call it being a victim—and others don't?

Beyond that, he entertained another burning question: If people could learn to be helpless, could they also unlearn it? Perhaps, he thought, there was a way, without years of therapy or drugs, to teach depressed human beings to become happier people who could learn to thrive and flourish in the world around them.

In 1997, when Dr. Seligman was elected president of the American Psychological Association, he made it his mission to find out. With help from many of his colleagues, the seeds that were sown more than 30 years earlier germinated into the new field of positive psychology. If clinical psychology was satisfied to take people from a minus five to zero, positive psychology would get them from zero to plus five. And to give it the credibility it needed, the characteristics and boundaries of this new discipline would be deeply grounded in science.

Today, some of the most influential psychologists in the country are researching, experimenting, and publishing studies on the science of happiness, including scientists such as Daniel Gilbert, PhD, of Harvard; Daniel Kahneman, PhD, of Princeton; Shelley Taylor, PhD, of the University of California, Los Angeles; Edward Diener, PhD, of the University of Illinois; and Becca Levy, PhD, of Yale. You will see these names and read examples of the studies put forth by these and other equally prominent scientists as you continue through this book.

A Tale of Love and Optimism

My own foray into positive psychology—in the mid 1980s—happened long before the movement as we know it today had been conceived. I suppose I was ripe for a change in thinking, but in effect, all it took was the story of a single patient.

I had been working as a medical psychologist at Canyon Ranch in the Life Enhancement Center, which is a goal-directed, health-enhancement program. It differs from a fun and fitness vacation, which is what the spa is about. At the time, I had been practicing the conventional way—that is, drawing out the details of a patient's problems and then exploring them together. One afternoon, a remarkably upbeat older woman named Barbara came to see me. She had come because, having just been named to the board of the Life Enhancement Center, she was interested in what we were doing there. She seemed quite interested in our methods, so I decided that instead of telling her how we work, I would demonstrate the ways we brought out people's strengths and examined the possibilities in their lives. I put on my psychologist's hat and got right to it.

As we talked, she told me stories that included situations that might have pushed even the strongest person into a state of despair. She had lived for years with an alcoholic husband, who was a womanizer and often an embarrassment to the family, but she loved him dearly until the day he died, and she had no reservations about saying so. She had survived a harrowing bout with cancer and, worst of all, had lost her beloved son years earlier in the Korean War. "But," she said, "I have two other wonderful children whom I adore and see often and a business I have gone to almost every day of my life."

Listening to her language and watching her demeanor, you couldn't help but conclude that although she had weathered some pretty treacherous storms, those storms hadn't dampened her enthusiasm for life. She was a strong, capable woman who knew what she valued and understood what was important. She had been subjected to trials and tribulations in life but still found a great deal of fulfillment, meaning, and purpose in living.

Perseverance is an incredible and important component of the pursuit of happiness. Like most happy women, Barbara never gave up.

"Why do you think you are so happy?" I asked her that afternoon.

"Why wouldn't I be?" she answered. "I just sold my business, so now I can start to do the things I've always wanted to do." She still saw possibilities in her life. It mattered not at all to her that she was 86 years old.

That's when it dawned on me. If a woman like this, who had lived with an alcoholic husband and lost a son forever to war, could still be such a happy woman, there had to be a reason. Why, in the face of such heartbreak, was this woman still happy? I was determined to find out just what that reason was.

I pored through the literature—which was sparse on the subject at that time—and had discussions with my colleagues. Everyone brought something to the mix, but I learned the most, far and away, from the guests I counseled at Canyon Ranch. It was through the lens of their experiences that I first ventured into the realm of what brought people happiness, and I admit I was surprised by what I found. It didn't appear to be about money, because I learned that people of enormous wealth worry just as much about money as people with much, much less. Social status wasn't directly related to happiness, because it turned out that people of great status were often far lonelier than those whose names will never be known to anyone beyond their family and friends. It turned out, too, that people of power are as afraid of the world as those who are powerless. In the end, I learned that happiness is far more than a mood or an emotion; it is a way of being, a way of knowing what's right and good, and living true to that.

Can Happiness Be Defined?

Cognitive theorists say happiness is what you experience on the way to a goal. Hedonists say it comes with the realization of the goal itself. Most happiness researchers—and there appear to be hundreds these days—define happiness as a state of mind, or an emotion. It's considered one of the six major emotions, the others being surprise, fear, disgust, anger, and sadness. You'll notice that four of the six are negative (only surprise is neutral).

The definition of happiness doesn't really matter all that much. It changes from moment to moment anyway, depending on who is defining it and what experiences they are using as parameters. What is way more important than defining happiness is living it.

You've Got to Accentuate the Positive

We know from research that happier people are more successful, more hardworking, more socially engaged—and healthier—than those who are less happy. In other words, beyond the expected perks that come with a pleasant and flourishing life, happiness (which for the purposes of this book is interchangeable with positive emotions) is actually good for you. Other positive emotions—including hope, optimism, contentment, and gratitude—help us to grow. They help us solve problems, improve the quality of our relationships, and energize us for positive action. Positive emotions fuel resilience in the midst of adversity, which in turn helps resilient people bounce back more rapidly to their precrisis levels of functioning. And it is positive emotions that take us beyond the day-to-day business of surviving to the ultimate goal in life—thriving.

Negative emotions serve their purpose, too. Whoever wrote, "You've got to accentuate the positive, eliminate the negative" had it right—or almost right. While positive emotions help us thrive, it was negative emotions that helped us survive. Essentially, we need both.

Evolution and Emotions

It turns out that it's negative rather than positive thinking that has the deepest roots in humans. We are far more likely to remember what we did wrong than what we did right. For example, you may give the greatest speech of your life, but when it's over, you're more likely to recall—or beat yourself up about—the single flubbed sentence. We're more likely to remember what other people did wrong as well. When you're out on the highway, how often do you pick out the good drivers? I doubt that you ever think, *How nice that he's been driving perfectly straight and going a steady 65.* If you're like me, you focus on the one driver who cuts you off. And even though the offending driver is on your radar for just a few seconds, your heart rate soars, along with your blood pressure, for perhaps 10 more minutes.

It's a fact of life. You can take a metaphorical walk in the park forever and remain oblivious to the beauty surrounding you, but let just the tiniest blister develop on your smallest toe, and man, does that get your attention!

Right about now, you're probably thinking, *Okay, if positive emotions are so good for us and so important in our lives, why are we all so filled with negative ones?*

It's Evolutionary, My Dear Woman

It boils down to a single word: *survival.*

For all of our ancestors' adaptive successes, evolution is probably the biggest reason that we tend to accentuate the negatives in our lives. It's why we compare ourselves, our homes, and our children to everyone else's and rarely win. It's why we strive for perfection that we will never attain. It's why we can't always forgive when we should, and why, although we may become happy, we don't stay that way for very long. It's also why, as you'll soon see, we so often fall into the negative traps that obstruct our desire for happiness.

Man as a species evolved during the Neolithic Age, 80,000 to 120,000 years ago (depending on whom you ask). While modern man has been around for at least 80,000 years, our capacity to be civil has been around for only 10,000 years, which is when the frontal lobes of the brain began to develop.

We humans actually have three brains. The most primitive of the brains, which goes back 4 million years in the forerunners of human beings, is the reptilian brain. It comprises the brainstem and lower brain and is similar to what is seen in reptiles like snakes, hence its name. The reptilian brain has a single focus: survival. It doesn't think, and it doesn't sense emotions. It is responsible only for those elements that keep us going: fight or flight, hunger and fear, attack or run. It operates purely at the level of stimulus-response. The reptilian brain is what makes a woman scream, "Save me!" and jump onto a chair at the sight of a mouse—without even taking time to consider that the chair is a $500,000 Louis XIV antique.

We share our midbrain, called the mammalian or limbic brain, with the animals that came along after reptiles—mammals. This brain is responsible for, among other things, the desire to run in packs. Because humans weren't faster or stronger than many of the predators in the world, they found their strength in cohesive numbers. They had no choice but to band together. For example, in the African jungle, a troop of chimpanzees can be a formidable force, whereas a single chimp might easily be lunch. So while the reptilian brain is all about "me," the mammalian brain is about "me" but also about "we." A most significant aspect of the mammalian brain is that it is the seat of emotions like love, anger, compassion, jealousy, and hope.

Ten thousand years ago, man developed a higher-order thinking brain, and for the first time, we had decency, civility, morality, and law coming into play. This third brain—the neocortex ("new" cortex)—rests over the limbic brain (which is in turn atop the reptilian brain) and is responsible for our intelligence. It is called upon to process abstract thought, words and symbols, logic and time. It is because of this higher-order moral brain that we have civility, or civilization.

Thus, you see that even before there was intelligence, there were emotions. Of all the survival emotions our ancestors left behind as a legacy, the most prominent were the negative ones: anger, sadness, and most important, fear. Make no mistake: They needed these negative emotions.

Anger sent them after foes and reinforced their determination to win. Sadness slowed them down, thereby conserving energy they might later need. But it was fear that kept them safe, because fear heralded jeopardy. If they had not been safe, they wouldn't have been our ancestors! Fear was behind what we know today as the fight, flight, or freeze reaction to menace or threat.

At the time, each of these emotions helped ensure our ancestors' survival, and they remain part of our legacy today. If it was fear that was critical to survival in the Neolithic Age, it is still fear—of not having enough or being enough—that is the very reason that we are constantly fighting an uphill battle on the road to happiness. Again, men are more concerned with the fear of not having enough, while women fear that they are not enough.

Women probably had it the hardest in the past. They had to be attractive enough to get "the guy," clever enough to keep him from straying, fertile enough to bear his children, strong enough to bring home the berries, and resilient enough to make it through the icy winters. Back at the cave, women had two general tasks: looking after the young and keeping things running on the home front when the men were out on the hunt. Because these tasks were often mutually exclusive—even today, one can't always watch the children and get the chores done—women had to share the demands of everyday existence, which meant they had to develop strong interdependent relationships to support one another. This is why, even today, while men are power driven, women are so much about relationships.

Skiing through the Trees

In the end, we have evolution and our primitive brain to thank for our present state of affairs. We seem to have been saddled with the equivalent of continually looking over our shoulders for the approaching threat, or more familiarly, "waiting for the other shoe to drop."

I call this being hardwired for hard times, which means it doesn't matter if we are walking under the stars with a lover on a beach or shopping for a bargain in Filene's Basement, we keep looking for problems. And that's too bad because when problems become our focus, we lose sight of so much of the good that surrounds us.

It involves the same concept as glade skiing—skiing through a stand of closely spaced trees. The trick, any experienced instructor will tell you, is to avoid looking at the trees, because you literally move toward what you focus on. If you look at a tree, you'll start heading for it. Likewise, if you start looking for the worst, you'll find it, pure and simple. Instead, why not focus on the glade—the space between the trees—and head for that.

Yes, you're more naturally tuned in to threatening forces, but that doesn't mean you need to spend all your time focused on them. In fact, the more you can relegate those hardwired responses to background noise, the happier you will be. Just because we're stuck with certain unpleasant emotions—gifts from our ancestors neatly tied up with ribbons of fear—doesn't mean that we can't find a way of avoiding them on our journey toward a life full of contentment and joy.

Are Some of Us Happier Than Others?

It would seem so. In fact, many of us are happy in spite of our ancestors' legacy. Some of us are just plain born happy.

David Lykken, PhD, a researcher from the University of Minnesota, published a paper in 1996 that looked at the role of genes in determining happiness. He gathered information on 4,000 sets of twins born in Minnesota from 1936 through 1955 and compared happiness data for the identical twins with those for the fraternal twins. He looked at traits such as sunny disposition, easygoing personality, stress management, and levels of anxiety. He concluded that 50 percent of our life satisfaction comes from our genes, and he attributed 10 percent to circumstantial factors such as income, education, and marital status. The rest comes from "life's slings and arrows."

This genetic predisposition to happiness is what turned Dr. Lykken on to his theory of the happiness set point, which is similar to our weight set point. The set point means that eventually, despite positive or negative external factors, we tend to return to our predetermined happiness range, sometimes in a short amount of time.

This doesn't mean that you can't raise the set point, however. You can—even if you have a gene configuration for curmudgeonliness (although you may always be a somewhat of a curmudgeon). Nor does the set point mean that you can't learn to be a little more optimistic, a little more hopeful, a little more constructive, and a little more positive.

With just a small amount of effort, you can seed your own positive emotions by looking for positive meaning in current circumstances and strengths in yourself and others. You can influence your own happiness in many ways—and yes, you can become lastingly happier.

How to do it is what the rest of this book is all about.

CHAPTER TWO

Perfectionism: You Can't Get There from Here

There is no cosmetic for beauty like happiness.
Marguerite, Countess of Blessington

At 8:45 on a balmy September evening, with a low Miami moon slanting through her living room windows, Julie pulled a piano bench up to her baby grand and, in front of 22 of her closest friends, easily launched into the opening bars of Rachmaninoff's Piano Concerto No. 2. Julie was 47 and an avowed music lover who had been practicing the piano almost daily since she began taking lessons at the age of 9. But this evening was special. Until now, she had done her best to avoid having a listening audience of any size.

It wasn't because she wished to hide her talent. On the contrary. For decades, Julie had longed to share her music with those she loved. But it was out of the question. That is, until she faced down a lifelong demon—fear. You see, until that balmy Miami evening, she was terrified of making a musical mistake in front of anyone. Her fear involved nothing more serious than hitting a wrong note.

I first met Julie in the spring of 2004. She was a young-looking mother of two who, even with her somewhat serious demeanor, had a certain energy. She arrived at my office that afternoon straight from the tennis court, dressed in tennis whites and looking—in a healthy way—like she had just finished a few good sets. She pulled off her sun visor and shook out her hair before settling into one of the two chairs opposite my sofa. "Sorry I didn't get a chance to change," she said. "The tennis clinic ran a little late."

It's amazing to me how many women come to the office and apologize right up front for the way they look, as if I might expect them to be attired in a manner appropriate for 5th Avenue. My antennae perked up. Apologizing for wearing the wrong outfit when you're perfectly well dressed is one small perfectionist tendency. If I was right, if it turned out that perfectionism was Julie's cross to bear, I was willing to bet there would be at least three more apologies before the hour was over.

In my 20 years at Canyon Ranch, I've encountered this from dozens of women. I'm still waiting to hear a similar remark from a man.

I took the other chair. "What brings you here?" I asked.

"I probably shouldn't be taking up your time . . ." she began (second apology), and continued, "I mean, this is probably going to sound so insignificant . . . (translation: What I have to say is not good enough or important enough) . . . but, well, there is this one thing . . ." She looked down. "I have a problem playing the piano."

"I take it you *can* play, though."

"Oh, I can *play* all right. I play all the time. Just not in front of anyone." As she spoke, the fingers on her left hand moved ever so slightly, as if she were fingering an imaginary piano in her lap. "My music brings me so much happiness. I want to share it with my family and friends. But for some reason, I just can't do it."

I corrected her, "You mean you haven't done it yet. Tell me, is there anyone you play for?"

"Other than my teachers years ago? No one. Never."

"And if you try?"

"If I try, I lift my hands over the keys and they freeze. In midair. Like they were being held there by a string or something." Her eyes told me this issue was not as frivolous as she had led herself to believe.

"Any idea what's stopping you?"

"I'm scared."

Of course: fear. *The elephant in the room.* Fear of not being good enough. It's hardwired into our brains—thanks to our great-great-great-grandma and grandpa's need to stay alive in the face of impending disaster. Fear that has resided comfortably in our brains for so long, it has no intention of being uprooted. I asked her what she was afraid of.

"Of making a mistake. Of hitting the wrong key. Of ruining the piece." Her fingers stopped moving. "Playing the piano should be about the *music.* For me, though, it's all about the performance." She shook her head. "I just don't get it."

Maybe she didn't get it, but I did. Julie expected perfection from herself, nothing less. And if she couldn't have it, she'd rather have nothing. Thank goodness the great pianists of every era had the courage to make mistakes. That goes for composers, too. If all composers were afflicted with this problem, there would be no music in the world. I don't even want to imagine what kind of world that would be.

When a woman I am counseling appears to be basically happy, I often question her about what I consider the three most important elements of a full life: her relationships, her health, and her purpose. During the first hour I spent with Julie, I established that she was doing quite well on the first two counts but wasn't quite as strong in the purpose area. She had a happy marriage of 21 years, was successful in her real estate career, and appeared to be in good health. Despite all this, though, she was missing a component in her life that would make her feel happy and fulfilled. She wanted to do something that had great meaning to her. She wanted to share her music but couldn't because she was afraid of producing an imperfect result.

Fear. The hidden armature beneath the trap of perfection.

Perfectionism: A Driver or a Trap?

Perfectionism has two sides: It can be a driver or a trap. When perfectionism is a driver—sometimes referred to as normal perfectionism—it can provide the perfectionist with a real sense of pleasure from both striving for excellence and attaining it. The perfectionism itself often supplies the needed energy and meticulous attention to detail that leads to accomplishment. Perfectionism is what keeps writers at their desks, scientists at their benches, and artists in front of their canvases. Athletes also fit into this mold, and you can see it in the way an ice skater repeats the same triple Lutz over and over and over in practice until it is practically flawless. Gymnasts walk a balance beam for hours; competitive riders jump their horses to the point of exhaustion. But in the end, all that work pays off. In addition to getting their photos on Wheaties boxes, these athletes ooze self-esteem. Theirs is the type of perfectionism this country most cherishes because it reflects our culture's values of discipline, tenacity, positive attitude, and hope.

Perfectionism, however, can also be a trap in the real sense of the word, and that is the type we're addressing here. It's the type that keeps people from taking risks for fear of failure, that keeps them procrastinating for fear of making a mistake. Such people, although going perhaps to the outer limits of their potential, never feel a sense of satisfaction because in their eyes, they never do anything well enough.

In my observation, this type of perfectionism is far more pervasive in women than in men, and it comes in many guises. In youth, it has to do with our grades, how we score on the athletic field, who our friends are, and how we look—emphasis on the latter. Later in life, women seek other things: They convince themselves that they would be happy if only they were married to the perfect guy, lived in the perfect home, owned the perfect car, had the perfect children, took the perfect trip, had the perfect job— and okay, it wouldn't be so bad if they also looked like Angelina Jolie.

Well, the best words I can offer regarding this self-sabotaging trap are these: *Perfection is an illusion. You can't get there from here.* Of course, if it will make you feel better, neither can Angelina Jolie or the Jennifers—Aniston and Lopez—or Halle Berry or Queen Elizabeth, for that matter. So at least you're in good company.

People have a misperception about perfectionism: They think it's all about being the best. But hidden behind the illusion of being the best is a very flawed assumption. We think that by reaching the mythical level of perfectionism, we automatically attain security. If we were perfect, our lives would be totally manageable, absolutely predictable, and therefore completely secure. We would never have to worry about anything in life again. Think about it; if we never make a mistake, we will never embarrass ourselves. We will be safe and secure forever.

Well, that's all very well and good, except there's one huge flaw. *It ain't gonna happen.* We're creatures of flesh and blood. Much of the story of Genesis is about this very fact. We're never going to be perfect. You lose the 5 pounds you always dreamed of losing; now you want to lose 10. You get your face lifted; now you notice the vertical lines in your lips. You have three pars on the front nine; why couldn't you nail the fourth?

Who gets to belong to the sorority of perfectionists? Anyone can join. You simply have to subscribe to one or more of the following:

- Nothing I do or have is good enough.
- Events and experiences and how I look are good or bad, right or wrong, perfect or imperfect, with nothing in between.
- I have to register a performance "10" every time. If I can't do something perfectly, it's not worth doing.
- If I make a mistake, I've failed. And if I fail, I won't be accepted.
- Everyone but me achieves success with a minimum of effort.

Perfectionism has its costs, too. First of all, it's murder on your self-esteem, and second, it can be self-perpetuating. Here's what happens. You set an unreachable goal. Because the goal is unreachable, you fail to meet it. Failing leads you to self-criticism and self-blaming, which results in low self-esteem. Now you think you're not good enough, so you either give up on the original goal or set another one, thinking if you try harder this time, you will succeed. And of course, you don't. Instead, you just perpetuate the cycle, picking up stress, anxiety, and even depression along the way.

Why would anyone want to lay such a burden on herself? Why do some women believe they must be movie-star beautiful or the CEO of a major corporation to finally jump off that treadmill of dissatisfaction and take an emotional deep breath?

Why is good enough good enough for some of us and not for others?

Aha! The $64,000 question!

The answer isn't nearly as expensive.

What Leads to Perfectionism?

Three factors can probably lay claim to a large percentage of the responsibility. Our culture plays a large role. So does society. And of course, no explanation is complete if we don't lay at least some of the blame on our parents. But first things first: *their* parents.

The Evolutionary Component

Let's start with the evolutionary piece of the puzzle because this explains in large measure why perfectionism is so much of an issue for women.

Even though conditions that were once necessary to ensure survival are no longer present, much of perfectionism harks back to the early days, when certain resources were scarce. By "resources," I'm referring specifically to men. The premise was quite simple: If women wanted to survive, they needed men as partners. If they were to be well fed and protected and wrapped in furs, they needed someone to bring home the mammoth mignon. Most important, though, if they wanted to pass on their genes, *cherchez le homme.* In short, they needed guys. (Of course, we men needed women, too, but that's for another book.)

The resource pool—meaning the number of available men—was never all that large to begin with because in those days, humans lived in small groups. Sometimes that meant maybe a hundred to a tribe, and sometimes even fewer. A man's lifestyle was nothing short of treacherous in those days—trekking out in the cold, stalking beasts, wondering who would end up being dinner for whom. Many never returned from the hunt, and reaching 30 was roughly equivalent to hitting the century mark today. In the end, our foremothers may have had pretty meager pickings when it came to selecting mates. Clearly, competition was keen for the best of the pack.

Thus, it should come as no surprise that as a woman emerged from her cave, she probably took a good look at the woman in the cave next door and wondered, *How do I stack up against her?*

And herein lies the genesis of why today's woman constantly compares herself to other women.

Oh, I know. Today there are hundreds of thousands of men around for every man who survived the Ice Age. But consider that the number of available women has exploded as well. Nature has perpetrated a dirty little trick on women because even today, there are always more females around than males, with the gap widening as we age. And to put the frosting on the cake, many older men are still proudly collecting the decades-younger trophy wife.

While women may not have to look all that far to see the countenance of a Jake Gyllenhaal, a Tom Cruise, a Harrison Ford, or a Paul Newman, the problem is that every other woman is looking at them, too. Today's woman may be 80,000 years newer, but for her now, just as in the Stone Age, competition remains stiff—or so she believes. And if she's going to get the goods, she's got to look pretty good herself.

On behalf of my sex, I'll assume some of the blame for this because, while I'm not happy to admit it, what's the first thing that most guys look for in a woman? If you guessed intelligence, you go to the back of the class.

Here's Looking at You, Kid

I can talk until I'm blue in the face and try to convince you that looks shouldn't matter, but science will show both of us that they do. Arizona State University evolutionary psychologist Douglas Kenrick, PhD, and his colleagues concluded from their research that when all is said and done, men are attracted to good-looking women. No surprise there. But they've also shown that these beautiful faces can bring on some social problems as well. Dr. Kenrick discovered in his research that men exposed to multiple images of attractive women subsequently rated their commitment to their real-life partners as lower, compared with men exposed to average-looking women. (Women exposed to multiple images of dominant, high-status men showed a similar lessening in their commitment to their partners, compared with women exposed repeatedly to images of less dominant men.)

Another finding in the study was that women shown successive images of other women who are unusually attractive subsequently felt less attractive themselves and showed a decrease in self-esteem. Maybe that explains why, for example, a 50ish woman will go into a hair salon with a photo of Gwyneth Paltrow and ask for the same haircut. She doesn't just want the haircut; she wants to look like Paltrow, too.

The Cultural Component

If evolution explains the genesis of why women feel they must be perfect, our culture seems quite satisfied to perpetuate the situation, and in this case, it may have nothing whatsoever to do with attracting a man. It's also about being good enough and feeling secure with who you are.

Nowhere is the trap of perfectionism more rampant than in the way women view themselves from the vantage point of an outsider looking in.

Naomi Wolf, in her 2001 bestseller *The Beauty Myth*, describes the US beauty and fashion industry as a $100 billion-a-year business, with much of that money coming from advertisers and marketing psychologists. The job of these marketers, she says, is to make people feel "not right" unless they buy the consumer goods marketed to make them feel "right." The message is reinforced everywhere you look. You need earplugs and a blindfold to miss it. Who sponsors the Miss America Pageants? Revlon beauty products. Who sponsors *American Idol?* Diet Coke. You see the trend?

The body type of a Tyra Banks is found in 1 in 200,000 women, yet Tyra and her supermodel sister are held up as icons for every woman to emulate.

Who cares if the goal is unrealistic and unattainable? If 199,999 women are unhappy with themselves, that is just what cosmetics companies, spas, and plastic surgeons are looking for—they're worth billions.

A sign in a Los Angeles plastic surgeon's office asks patients, "Are you satisfied with looking good when you can look great?" Certainly not! Not when there is such easy access to Botox, lasers, hyaluronic acid, and meso-therapy. Not when there are mini-tucks, maxi-tucks, tummy tucks, and *Nip and Tuck* (the wildly successful Fox TV series); not when there are face-lifts, liposuction, breast augmentation, and vein zapping. They're all out there, just waiting to be plucked from the tree of instant beauty (for a price, of course). The promise is always the same: Happiness is in the next product, procedure, or process. Just sign on the dotted line.

I have to applaud the Unilever Company, which uses "real models" to advertise its Dove products. The real, nonairbrushed images of these every-day size 14 American women clad in their bras and panties—heads lifted, wrinkles and rolls be damned—adorn billboards and buses from Vermont to California. *This is what real women look like!* As my wife says, "God bless 'em."

Not only does the culturally programmed myth of perfection ravage a woman's self-esteem, it can wreak havoc with her physical health as well. Many women—young girls in particular—suffer from devastating and often fatal eating disorders such as anorexia and bulimia because they feel that they aren't thin enough. Anorexia is characterized by starvation and compulsive exercising; bulimia is excessive concern over body weight that leads to binge eating and self-induced vomiting.

Cynthia Bulik, PhD, of Virginia Commonwealth University studied more than 1,000 female twins ages 25 to 65 to evaluate perfectionist traits and psychological problems. The study showed that perfectionism—most notably the tendency to view mistakes as personal failures—was signifi-cantly associated with anorexia and bulimia.

In his book *The Best Little Girl in the World,* Steven Levenkron tells the story of Casey, the all-American girl. An excellent student and a cheerleader, she never gave her parents a moment of concern. She was the perfect daughter—until she began to starve herself. Every girl or woman with this disorder that I've ever interviewed has allowed the cultural fixation with thinness to dominate her life and become her mantra. It's all driven by fear: fear of being fat, fear of food, fear of disappointing family, fear of losing control. I remember one very bright woman talking to her doctor about how she feared ingesting even germs because she was concerned about their calorie content. She had an IQ of 150, but intelligence is no match for the will of someone with anorexia. So sad.

In the end, it doesn't matter how much weight women with anorexia lose, it's never enough because they will always *feel* fat, i.e., imperfect. Anorexia is an attempt to control something (in this case, the woman's physical body) without hurting anybody else, thereby retaining the reputation of the best little girl in the world. Women with anorexia are universally blind to the pain and suffering their "benign" behavior causes their families.

An Obsession with Youth

Age is another issue that weighs heavily for women. Trying to shave off the decades is yet another way women sabotage themselves by setting themselves an impossible standard. The last time I was in an airport newsstand, I couldn't help but notice how young today's cover girls seem to be. (And no, it's not because I'm getting older. Not much, anyway.) Remember when Calvin Klein took heat for showcasing a group of boys and girls—most in their teens—wearing skimpy underwear in a billboard ad that stood high above Times Square in New York? He didn't get away with that one, but he sure did succeed when 13-year-old jeans-clad Brooke Shields stretched out across television screens all over the country and practically purred that "nothing comes between me and my Calvins." Of course, women of all ages ran out and bought them by the carload. Who doesn't want to look like that? I'll bet even Shields wants to look like she did at 13 again.

When did our society decide it's not okay to get older? I'm guessing that this obsession with youth all started around the decade of the 1960s. That's when women borrowed their daughters' clothes (instead of vice versa), and 70-year-old women wore long hair and short shorts. By the time of the Vietnam War, dungarees morphed into "jeans," the line between child and adult was blurred, and a whole generation was taught not to trust anyone over 30. So women turned into kids, kids stayed kids, and no one was watching the store.

It verges on disaster when a woman sets a goal of looking, feeling, and acting decades younger. I can't count the number of women who have sat across from me—intelligent women with many intrinsic qualities—who believe they're valued only on the basis of their physical beauty. "But it's transitory," I say. "It's nature. If you let that penetrate your psyche, you're going to keep your eyes on the clock, and every time it ticks, you'll think, 'Oh, my God, I'm aging!' Is that the kind of life you want?"

Of course, they say no.

But do they mean it?

That is just a small example of what I'm referring to when I say perfectionists trap themselves with impossible goals. The woman who says she'll be happy only if she looks and feels younger. Well, who can turn back the clock? And who would ever want to? If she can't come to acceptance, she'll be pushing that rock uphill forever.

Happy women flow gracefully into the next decade and the next because they find things to love about themselves throughout their life cycles.

I can't argue that women who go through cosmetic surgery don't experience a certain uplift—if you'll pardon the pun. But here's what happens: Plastic surgery can improve appearance only so much. Some, but far from all, cosmetic surgeons are smart enough to know that at some time, a woman reaches the point where she's had too much. More cosmetic surgery is not an alternative, and it's time to come to terms with reality.

Larry Robbins, MD, a plastic surgeon from Miami Beach, was particularly mindful that his technology went only so far. When women returned again and again for more surgery, he never hesitated to turn them down if he believed they had had enough. He told me once that many of the women he turned down went to other local surgeons who were only too happy to comply with their wishes, but he never regretted his decisions, ever.

Recently, researchers at Yale provided a highly compelling reason to look positively on getting older. Becca Levy, PhD, of the Yale School of Public Health has been investigating the way certain psychosocial factors influence the way we age. In a study, the results of which were published in the *Journal of Personality and Social Psychology,* she demonstrated scientific proof that how a person *perceives* getting older can directly affect longevity. The study goes back 23 years, with the sample consisting of 660 Ohioans ages 50 and older. The results showed that people with more positive perceptions of aging lived 7.5 years longer than those with negative perceptions. The differences Dr. Levy refers to include thinking such as, "Oh, my God, my skin is sagging. I have age spots. Digestive problems. I can't remember anything anymore . . ." as opposed to cherishing the freedom to go and do and climb mountains and dance at their granddaughter's wedding. She states as well that this advantage remained after age, gender, socioeconomic status, loneliness, and functional health were taken into consideration.

Now if that isn't a reason to celebrate your 50th, 60th, and 70th birthdays—and beyond—what is? To me, there is nothing I enjoy more than seeing an octogenarian who is cool and unflappable and at peace with herself and her age. It's wonderful.

The Psychological Component

As if the evolutionary and sociocultural aspects of perfectionism weren't enough, women are also saddled with a psychological element. Here is where women like Julie come into the picture.

Julie's fears were all about not measuring up. Not measuring up to *whom,* she didn't know. She simply felt she wasn't good enough. In effect, she was competing against herself, and the minute you start doing that, you freeze. Her feelings about not being good enough came from somewhere, but I had a hunch we were never going to find out exactly where that was. And I knew it didn't matter.

Perfectionist tendencies are an attempt to win love, acceptance, and approval. They often begin early in life, with our parents. Trying hard to live up to a parent's expectations is a common feature of perfectionism.

When love is conditional, girls try to do everything perfectly to avoid being judged or rejected. As a result, they grow up valuing themselves only on the basis of other people's approval, so self-esteem is based primarily on external standards. This trait is far less commonly found in boys because boys tend to be more competitive and thus more achievement oriented, and when you achieve, that's what feeds self-esteem. If they're not good at football, they become good at chess; if they're not good at chess, they become good with computers. And so it goes.

Women can't do that as well because they get stuck, hung up. I recently visited an adult-education writing class at Dartmouth College, and it was filled with very bright men and women. The instructor gave the students a 15-minute writing exercise in class. They were to write on a specific topic that happened to be nonfiction. Immediately afterward, they were given the opportunity to read their work aloud. All did so except Cindy, a young woman of about 30 who was good at poetry but not at nonfiction. I watched her agonize while the others were writing, and in the end, she refused to read, almost in tears, because, she told the class, she couldn't compete with what they had done. Instead of asking herself, *What are my strengths as a poet?* and then transferring them to writing nonfiction, she said her work was horrible, terrible, awful. She was frozen by the comparison. Her self-esteem was at rock bottom. She told me after class that she was the daughter of a Holocaust survivor and that her father had only once told her his story. I asked her if she had a passion for that story, and she said yes. I said, "Then that's the story you need to write." Fear had frozen her. She was engaged in that negative self-dialogue, saying, *All these people wrote so much better than I did, and I can't do it.*

Such beliefs create women who are vulnerable and excessively sensitive to the opinions and criticism of others, particularly their mothers. No matter how much women know it shouldn't be important, what their mothers think matters. A lot.

Janice, 45, flew from Buffalo to Miami Beach to visit her mother, whom she hadn't seen in 6 months. When she arrived at her mother's high-rise apartment building, her mother wasn't home, so Janice let herself into the apartment, put on a bathing suit, and went for a swim in the pool. An hour later, wearing a stretched-out T-shirt to cover her bathing suit and with wet hair clinging to the sides of her face, she returned to the apartment. Her mother, who had come home in the meantime, opened the door, took one look at her daughter, and said, "Well, I hope none of my friends saw you looking like this." Not "Hello!" Not "How great to see you!" Not even "Thanks for coming."

Is it any wonder that Janice is on her third round of plastic surgery? What are the chances she'll ever feel good about herself?

Happy women know that their worth is not determined by what they have or how they look but rather by successful relationships and emotional well-being.

The Joys of Getting It Wrong

Many of our greatest undertakings are accomplished while striving to better ourselves. Consider the scientists, artists, athletes, and successful businesspeople mentioned earlier in this chapter, who push themselves beyond their limitations in an attempt to be and do better. The reason they don't fall into the trap of perfectionism is that they are willing to make mistakes and risk failure. They see mistakes and imperfections as part of the reality of being human rather than as something to beat themselves up over.

The truth is, we'll make plenty of mistakes if we venture beyond our comfort zone, but that means we are calling on ourselves to grow and become more dynamic, and if we do this well, the end result is self-actualizing. Life, and everything that happens in the context of life, is an experiment. There's no doubt that some of the results of experimentation can be difficult and painful. But like the dogs in the study by Martin Seligman, PhD, mentioned in Chapter 1, do we hunker down and freeze, staying stuck, or do we get going, jump in new directions, and at least some of the time, find the benefits and rewards of living such a life?

Failure can be a teacher and the source of personal growth. Experiencing failure shows you have the strength to accept life's challenges. Failure is an opportunity to discover that success may be just around the corner if you're willing to take that first step.

The only true failure is quitting.

The Impostor Syndrome

In trying to show the world they're perfect, some women become open to what is known as the impostor syndrome. It occurs when a person who is genuinely competent is beset by a subjective sense of "faking others out." The perfectionist who succumbs to this believes that she is truly not good enough and that it's only a matter of time before she is found out. If she gives a speech, she's certain that some people in the audience will know she really doesn't know what she's talking about—even if in fact she is an authority on the subject. If she does experience success, she attributes it to good luck rather than ability. The problem is, the person with impostor syndrome lives with a fulltime fear that she may be exposed at any time—and the more successful she is, the greater her inner stress.

Psychologists Pauline Clance and Suzanne Imes first documented the impostor syndrome in 1978. They studied a group of successful, high-achieving women and found that many of them could not internalize their success; they just didn't believe they had earned it. A check of these beliefs proved that they were actually bright women who had received many awards or promotions on their own merits.

When Perfectionism Runs Amok

Perfectionism can work in reverse, too. I remember a young woman who came to see me complaining about not being able to find the right guy. She was very attractive and very smart and had a high-visibility job where she encountered a lot of eligible men. But nobody was perfect enough. This one didn't dress right, that one wasn't educated in the right institution of higher learning; one liked sports too much, another wasn't clean enough. She always looked for what was wrong with the men she dated—and found it, of course.

This was perfectionism run amok because until this woman finds the perfect man, she's essentially going to be single. Her homework was to go home and look in the mirror, long and hard. When she came back the next day, I asked, "What did you see?"

She said, "Well, my hair could use a coloring and my jeans are a little . . ."

I stopped her. "No, no. That's not what I meant. What did you see *inside*?"

She smiled. "Oh . . . inside?" She thought a moment and then said, "Well, I guess I'm kind of uptight. I'm moody sometimes. And I suppose I could be a little nicer . . ."

"So you're an imperfect woman looking for the perfect man," I said. "What are your odds?"

"Not very good," she decided, and we spent the hour discussing her fallibilities. To list them here would be beside the point. Suffice it to say that by listing them herself, she heard herself admitting that she was less than perfect and began to open her eyes to reality.

Happy women know that admitting a problem exists is the first step toward changing it.

A corollary to "I'm perfect, and therefore no one who is less than perfect is good enough for me" is "I should have married my college boyfriend." After spending the most important time and energy in life pursuing a career, many women awaken to the fact that they had a chance to marry someone many years previously but didn't for whatever reason. In the ensuing time, they have idealized this guy and spent additional time and energy fancifully trying to rewrite history and beating themselves up for dismissing the proverbial "McDreamy."

Nothing could be more counterproductive. It detracts from time and energy that could be devoted to something more constructive, and worse, it pits you against yourself. Can't you see the opening line? "Hello, I'm looking for someone to love me, because I *don't* love me." That concept reminds me of Groucho Marx's line, "I wouldn't want to belong to any club that would have someone like me as a member."

Can Women Caught in the Trap of Perfectionism Change?

Of course—but only if they want to.

It takes courage to overcome perfectionist tendencies because it requires admitting that you are human—and to be human is to be imperfect. It also means being willing to acknowledge what is actually true anyway, and that is that you've made mistakes all along the way in life, and possibly the biggest mistake of all is being driven to be a perfectionist. With understanding, you can easily challenge the self-defeating thoughts and behaviors that fuel perfectionism, and by employing some or all of the following tools, you can definitely make your life happier. But I must warn you, it takes a lot of courage.

Kaizen: The Perfectionism Antidote

If you have fallen into the trap of perfectionism, the most useful tool I know to get yourself out is based on a Japanese method called Kaizen. *Kaizen* is a Japanese word for continual improvement through small, incremental, and sometimes insignificant steps. You want to be smarter on a certain topic? Start with a single course, or a book, or a discussion with someone who knows at least a little more than you do. One small step is far better than no step at all. Do you think Toyota jumped from those boxy little square cars they produced in the 1970s to the much-lauded Lexus of today? No way. There were thousands and thousands of small steps, trials and errors, mistakes and corrections along the way.

I learned about this method—although I don't think it had a name back then—when I was studying for my doctorate in psychology 24 years ago. Every doctoral program has a time limit of about 7 years, during which you must prepare your thesis, write it, and defend it in front of a dissertation committee. During that period, I had had three false starts with three different topics. After uncountable hours spent researching, I just couldn't pull off any of them to my satisfaction. And time was running out for me.

In a bit of a panic, I called my friend and mentor Alan Bayer, PhD, who at the time was the chairman of the department of sociology at Virginia Polytechnic Institute in Blacksburg. When I explained my situation, he said he'd help if I'd buy lunch.

Three days later, over corned beef sandwiches at the local delicatessen, he got right to the point. "I know exactly what your problem is, Dan," he said. "You're trying to write the perfect paper! If you had all the money in the world and 10 lifetimes, you couldn't do the projects you're talking about. Remember, a dissertation is meant to be a contribution to the literature, not a recipe for world peace or the cure for cancer."

He was right, of course. I was afraid of sitting in front of that dissertation committee and being told, "Nope, not good enough." I saw all those years of hard work going up in smoke, and I told him so.

"Okay," he said. "Here's what you do. Think of a topic in which you have a keen interest, preferably with no more than 12 articles written on it, and no less than 6. Then read everything related that you can find and decide to write a paper that's this much better than what's out there." He illustrated "this much" by holding up his hand and separating his thumb and forefinger by a fraction of an inch.

It Only Has to Be This Much Better!

What a gift! When he put it in that context, I realized he was right. I didn't have to set the world on fire. I only had to do "this much" better. And that is one of the best tools I have ever seen for beating perfectionism back into the woods.

I took his advice. I found my topic and wrote my thesis, and I successfully defended it 7 months later. I had never heard of Kaizen before, and perhaps he hadn't either, but he was employing the philosophy to the letter. I'll always be grateful for his help.

Many women have told me they want to be writers but are afraid to start for fear they aren't good enough. You know the litany: "I'll never find a publisher. No one will want to read it. I don't have any important ideas. . . ." First of all, even if you write a bad book, you're still writing—and no doubt improving as you do so. For God's sake, don't set Ernest Hemingway as your standard. Set yourself as your standard and be a better writer today than you were yesterday. If you start now, you will be. I promise. And that is the mindset of Kaizen.

Perfectionism creeps into all aspects of life. There is no more important responsibility than raising children, so it's no surprise that women are sensitive to anything that suggests they did less than 110 percent for their kids. Forget it! No one can be über-mom 24/7, but you can be a "good-enough" mom who gets better at it as you go along.

The Pareto Principle

Somewhat different from Kaizen but in the same spirit is the Pareto principle. This principle hypothesizes that 20 percent of our efforts deliver as much as 80 percent of our results—meaning that the remaining 80 percent of effort delivers only 20 percent of results. So consider this: If 20 percent is enough to deliver a reasonably acceptable job—maybe not perfect but certainly well above adequate—then the remaining 80 percent of the time spent seeking perfection is wasted on a very small gain. The message? It's okay to produce a degree of perfection rather than absolute perfection. This is another great tool. Remember it.

More Tools to Combat Perfectionism

- **Be aware of the difference between setting high personal standards and perfectionism.** Setting high standards involves establishing reasonable goals in pursuit of success, while perfectionism involves setting impossibly high goals and is motivated by the fear of failure.

- **Change how you talk to yourself.** Keep your self-talk realistically positive: "It may take me a while, but I do get things done." Or instead of complaining that you never have time anymore to call your friends, for example, commit to calling one friend within the next 24 hours. Set the place and time so it will work.

- **When you find yourself obsessing about how you look, ask yourself these or similar questions.**

  What have my looks done for me?
  Am I only about my looks?
  Am I also smart or a kind, warm, nice person?
  Do I have a good personality?
  How many times today has my heart beat flawlessly?
  Has my immune system kept me well today?
  How am I feeling now that I have completed a great report?

- **Understand that the most important thing about falling into the compete-and-compare trap is that you always lose.** The best question is: What would it take to *win* today? Another of my mentors (I was lucky enough to have six), Robert Eliot, MD, an internationally known cardiologist, was fond of asking his patients,

"Are you winning?" If they hesitated or needed clarification or wanted to know in what context, he got the answer. Dr. Eliot believed that when people who are truly winning in life are asked that question, they unhesitatingly answer with a resounding "Yes!"

- **Learn to set realistic goals for yourself by looking closely at what you do best and beginning to build on that.** If you can easily run a mile, and your goal is to run 3, go for 1.1 miles the next few times out rather than 2 miles, which might be too hard and cause you to give up running altogether. If you want to lose weight, go for a 5-pound loss and celebrate when you get there. Then reassess and maybe consider losing another 5.

This last tool touches on the principle of Kaizen and is what seems to have helped Julie overcome her problem. So how did it happen that she could actually perform in front of all those people on that tropical night?

During her week at Canyon Ranch, I made sure she focused on what she *could* do—play the piano beautifully—rather than what she couldn't—play in front of people. Next, I convinced her that even the best pianists make mistakes, and nothing happens. Furthermore, I suggested that being the generous person she is, there was probably no greater gift she could give her family and friends than something as personal as sharing a moment of herself and her love of music. In short, I coached her to make this about others—others she loved—and not herself.

But then came her homework (most people who spend a week with me go home with homework). She had one assignment: to practice the art of Kaizen. We decided that she would play for someone she knew well and was comfortable around but who she believed wouldn't judge her at all. Then she was to increase her audience bit by bit. First, she selected her son's babysitter.

She had the babysitter stand in the kitchen and listen while she played the first piece. When "nothing happened," she allowed her to move into the living room. Three days later, she invited her repairman to join the audience. Within a few weeks, she was playing for her sister and finally her husband.

By the end of the month, Julie was ready to play for her friends, and she did so exquisitely. I learned of the performance in a letter from her that contained a tape. She explained in the letter that her husband had left a spray of roses on the piano and had slid a mini-recorder beneath it to tape her performance.

I love Rachmaninoff—especially the 2nd concerto. And with Julie playing, the notes sounded polished and beautiful. But if you really want to know the truth, my joy came not at all from the melody. It was the sustained reverberation of all those hands clapping in the end that was music to my ears.

CHAPTER THREE

Wanton Wanting: The Myths and Burdens of Affluence

Success is getting what you want.
Happiness is wanting what you get.

Dale Carnegie

Suze Orman, a financial expert and author, calls money and happiness two of the most prevailing forces in our lives. But, she says, "What's so interesting is how we've convinced ourselves that there is a powerful connection between them. We seem to believe that if we're rich, our lives will be perfect."

The truth is, not only is there *not* a strong relationship between affluence and happiness, the two may not even be loosely linked.

Over the years, I've counseled people of affluence and people barely scraping by, and I can tell you that money and all its trappings neither create nor sustain happiness. In fact—and here is where it becomes a trap—it can, and often does, do just the opposite.

Hard to believe? It shouldn't be, if you take into account that over the past 50 years, Americans appear to have bought lock, stock, and summer home into what I call the myths of affluence.

Myth #1: Money Can Buy Security

It would make life so easy if this were true, but you know as well as I do that security is not for sale.

Here's a hypothetical: You are a freelance writer and have invited an editor out for lunch, praying she'll assign you a coveted article in the Sunday *New York Times Magazine*. You call and make a reservation for two at the Grill Room of the Four Seasons Restaurant, knowing that it's going to set you back a bundle but also that it's where everyone who is *anyone* in publishing goes for lunch. You decide it's worth the gamble.

When the big day arrives, you put on your new suit, check that your credit card is in your wallet, and hail a taxi. Nervously, you walk alone into the restaurant, lifting your chin into the air to project just the right amount of confidence. Trying to hide your insecurities, you smile sweetly as you tip the tuxedoed maître d' $20. He nods effortlessly before leading you up a flight of stairs to a table in the balcony. *The BALCONY? You can't sit in the balcony! Only tourists sit in the balcony!! The balcony is Siberia! Your career—such as it was—is over.*

What, you wonder, did you do wrong? Was it your outfit? The tip? The chin tilt? What?

It was probably nothing. Maybe the main floor is reserved for the regulars. Maybe $20 wasn't enough for him. Maybe he just didn't know you. It doesn't matter. The point is, you had all the right accoutrements. You were out for lunch with an editor from the most prestigious American newspaper at one of the finest restaurants in New York. And you ended up embarrassed and miserable about the whole affair.

That's because no matter what we have or where we go, we carry with us those nagging survivalist fears that have been hardwired in our brains for generations: the fears of not having enough and not being enough. In fact, one of the principal concepts the science of happiness conveys about money is this: *Nobody ever thinks they have enough.*

Most of human evolution took place in a world of great danger and scarcity. There was never enough food to sustain a group for very long. Life was one incessant search for the basics. It was a necessary function of adaptation to look beyond the next hill or around the bend for food, shelter, or water. If the men brought home a huge beast, the feast was good for only a day or two before it spoiled, and then the hunters were off to the wilds to hunt again. That left our foremothers, insatiable gatherers all, to urgently forage for nuts and berries, always carrying with them that niggling feeling of scarcity—we need more, more, *more!*

As far as our brains know, we're still hunters (the men) and gatherers (the women) looking to stock the larders of our caves, even if today those larders take the form of Sub-Zero refrigerators. And how does today's woman gather?

She shops, of course!

Technically, today's women are emulating what their sisters did 80,000 years ago, but instead of doing it in a cranberry bog, they're doing it in places like Whole Foods and Bloomingdale's—the sensation of not having enough still very much in evidence. If you don't believe me, just go to the first floor of Macy's on the Friday after Thanksgiving.

Happy women understand that no matter what they own,
they will always feel a bit insecure about having
enough and being enough, but they don't let
these feelings rule their lives.

What Happy Women Know

Some years ago, a group of post-kidney-transplant patients came to Canyon Ranch, sent by a renal transplant surgeon of great renown whose institute was in Philadelphia. The surgeon had been a guest at the ranch, and when he saw all the possibilities it offered, he decided to try an experiment. Believing that post-transplant patients would be hugely benefited by having access to an exercise program, healthy meals, and perhaps some counseling—things that were not available in his institution—he offered a 2-week stay to a group of 10 patients, with an eye toward evaluating their recuperation and well-being compared with patients who were not offered this opportunity.

All of the patients were from different socioeconomic strata than our usual guests. I was in the spa lobby that morning and overheard a woman, who I later learned was named Grace, as she entered. Looking around, she turned to a fellow patient and whispered, "I shouldn't be here as a guest. I should be washing the windows."

The staff worked for 2 weeks with these patients, and by the end of their stay, they were eating better, moving their bodies better, and clearly feeling better overall. You could see it in their faces and the way they carried themselves. I spent an hour a day in counseling with Grace, who it turned out had been taught all her life to take care of others. My mission was to teach her the importance of first caring for herself and then giving to others.

One evening toward the end of her stay, I was having dinner in the dining room. She came in by herself, and I watched as the hostess led her to the Captain's Table, where people who come alone to the ranch gather to meet and socialize with other single guests. Five women, tanned faces aglow, jewels flashing, were already seated at the table. Grace told me the next day that halfway through the meal, several of the women began complaining about the inadequacy of the wait staff. "Eventually they all chimed in, whining that the service was too slow. Personally," she said, "I think they were annoyed because the waitress wasn't catering to them as though they were the only people in the room."

"I hope it didn't spoil your dinner," I said.

"Actually, Dr. Baker, you would have been proud. I decided to speak up—a first for me. I said, 'Have any of you ever waited tables? Do you know how *hard* a job that is? Do you know how *lucky* we all are to be sitting here being served?'"

I *was* proud of her. "What was their reaction to that?" I asked.

She told me that as soon as she said it, the women fell silent. "It was as though they were not at all sure about what they had said. Like deflated balloons. Almost unsure of what they should do next."

"And what did they do?"

"Nothing. I changed the subject and kept right on talking. Soon the others joined in, and we started to talk about all the good things we had learned from coming here and how we were going to keep it up when we got home. Then we just talked mostly girl-talk, you know?"

The point is, here was a woman who, while feeling somewhat out of her element, sat down at a table with strangers and was able to speak her truth. Even though she wasn't adorned with the trappings of wealth, she said what she believed was right. People who have lived through hard times usually grow as a result of their hardships and feel less fearful and more secure. Grace's confidence had grown in the short time she was here. That night, she was a happy woman, and I'd be willing to bet she still is.

Myth #2: Money Can Buy Happiness

"Whoever said money can't buy happiness doesn't know how to spend it."
—Lexus ad

"Happiness is right inside."
—Macy's catalog advertising shoes, shirts, and pocketbooks

"The second piece of pie or the second $50,000 never tastes as good."
—David G. Myers, PhD

For years, studies have shown that as long as their basic needs are met, the majority of people worldwide, regardless of age, race, or socioeconomic status, appear to be relatively happy. What's more, the same studies report, money does not make people happier. It can pay for certain services to make life easier, and it can even support some interesting experiences, but research tells us quite clearly that money buys neither happiness nor unhappiness. Here are the results of some of the more frequently cited studies.

- In 1958, America's average per capita income expressed in today's dollars was $9,000. Today the average is $20,000, so we're twice as rich, but we're not twice as happy. In fact, teen suicides have quadrupled and divorce rates have doubled in this period, and there is a growing incidence of depression, self-mutilation, and substance abuse.
- A 1978 landmark study presented evidence that both lottery winners and paraplegics adapted to their dramatic life changes within several months. The lottery winners initially experienced a huge jolt of elation, but it didn't last. Likewise, it took a while for the paraplegics to adapt to their new circumstances, but then they too returned to their previous levels of happiness.
- In 2004, 50 people on *Forbes* magazine's list of 100 wealthiest Americans were questioned and found to be only slightly happier than the average American.

Happiness, it turns out, is not the result of finally having it all but of appreciating what you have and enjoying the process of continuing achievement.

So, wake up, America! Happiness is not for sale.

You want more proof? Okay, put down this book for a minute and make a list of all the things that truly bring you joy, then count them. How many things on your list are available for purchase? That's what I thought.

So, despite the studies, why do we believe just the opposite? Because we're continually being bombarded with directives that tell us if we buy a product, we'll be happy. If we buy more of it, we'll be happier. Conversely, if we're not happy, it's probably because we haven't bought enough of it— whatever *it* is.

Everywhere we turn, we find the implication that "Happiness is your next purchase." The purpose of an ad is to make us feel inadequate and insecure. Then, miraculously, the same ad claims it can *solve* our insecurity by offering us products that can't fail. Brand X hair color will make us look younger, Brand Y shampoo will make us smell cleaner, and Brand Z dog food will make our dog's breath more pleasing. What more can we ask for?

When it comes to marketing, the folks on Madison Avenue are much smarter than we are. Why else would they pay Catherine Zeta-Jones whatever they pay her to smile out from the center of a double-page spread in the Sunday *New York Times*, coolly suggesting with those gorgeous eyes that we purchase T-Mobile phone service? Why not employ just some regular, everyday Jane? What, will someone please tell me, is the connection between a cell phone and Catherine Zeta-Jones? Did she invent it? Does she manufacture it? No. What the company wants you to think is that if you subscribe to this service, you will *look like* Catherine Zeta-Jones, or at the very least, if you're a man and you subscribe, perhaps she will shed Michael Douglas and marry *you* (but don't count on it).

Playing the Comparison Game

Some people believe that what you have in absolute terms doesn't have as much impact on your happiness as what you have compared to everyone else. It's that ancient brain of ours that keeps us running, always glancing over our shoulders to see what our neighbor has and then comparing our possessions to hers. The minute we get the first house, we want the second. The more we get, the more we need to boost our happiness level. We always want to be and have the best—which may be why our species dominated all the others.

When women compare themselves to other women, one of two things can happen, and neither is good. Most often (this is far and away the more common tendency), when a woman compares herself to someone else, she loses, which is rough on the self-esteem. The second outcome of comparison is that she "wins," which is likely to create another problem—arrogance. And of course, the outcome of arrogance is that it so often isolates you from other human beings.

> Happy women don't play the comparison game,
> because they know there will always be someone
> who has more than they do.

In one well-known study, a group of MBAs were asked this question: "Would you rather make $100,000 when everyone around you makes $120,000, or make $90,000 when everyone around you makes $70,000?" Surprisingly—or maybe not so surprisingly—a majority opted for the lower salary, but only if everyone at the company knew about the discrepancy.

In Tim Kasser's book *The High Price of Materialism*, a strikingly similar quotation appears, this time concerning Jim Clark, an executive at Silicon Graphics and later the founder of Netscape and Healtheon.

> Before Silicon Graphics, Clark said, a fortune of $10 million would make him happy; before Netscape, $100 million; before Healtheon, a billion; now, he [said] "Once I have more money than Larry Ellison, I'll be satisfied." Ellison, the founder of the software company Oracle, is worth $13 billion.

Myth #3: Happiness Is Infinite

Using happiness as bait—buy now/fly later—works best when we believe that the happiness will go on forever.

I'm so sorry to disappoint you, but the truth is, *no, it won't.*

That's because the human brain quickly becomes conditioned to positive experiences. Our newest possessions make us happy for only a certain period of time before our brains become used to them. Then we need more to restore that happiness summit, only to adapt to *those* pleasures and head out in search of the next high. Think about it. How long is your happiness sustained after you get a raise? If you're like most people, within a 2-month period, you've adapted to the extra money and are already lusting after the next raise. Positive psychologists call this concept—that an increase in wealth creates an increase in satisfaction for only a short time—the accommodation theory. Economists label it the hedonic treadmill.

The term *hedonic treadmill* was coined in an often-cited essay in 1971 by psychologists Philip Brickman and Donald Campbell, who showed through their landmark research that by the time people recalibrate their happiness levels to the improved circumstances, the improvements are no longer considered special. In other words, as with the elation of the lottery winners and the tragedy of the paraplegics, good things make us only temporarily happy. So do bad things. African Masai appear to be as happy living in dung huts without plumbing or electricity as I am on my ranch. The theory runs amok, however in certain instances, such as when material wants prove insatiable. Case in point: Imelda Marcos, living a life of grandeur among the poverty of her fellow Filipinos, would never have enough shoes. Martha Stewart risked reputation and jail time for what to her was most likely the paltry sum of $45,000. Unfortunately for her, she lost on both accounts.

Can't Buy Me Love

Myth #3 tells us happiness is infinite, but you've seen that it is far from that. Even nature has jumped on the bandwagon here. Let's return to the Stone Age once more, only this time, let's look at the principles of pleasure. Two of them fit right into the myth of happiness being infinite.

Then, as now, pleasure came from things that were good for our survival, particularly the two life essentials—food and sex. Food because it kept us from starving to death, and sex because it was the way to propagate the human race. Unlike trinkets we can purchase at the drop of a dollar (not many of them around any more), the pleasure derived from both food and sex was designed by nature to be transient. That is, *not to last*. Goodbye infinity. The experience of pleasure in these two cases virtually ensures repetition. If the pleasure one got from eating or from sex were infinite, you would have to do them only once. What would that do to the restaurant business? What would it do to the wedding planners?

There isn't a single culture in the world whose celebrations don't involve food. This was true even in the death camps. People would hoard food and have a little celebration for a birthday or a holiday. My father-in-law was in a POW camp, and he often recounted stories about how he and his fellow prisoners would skimp on their already meager rations just to save something in order to have a Christmas party or a Thanksgiving feast. It was far from a feast, but comparatively speaking, it was far more than what they were accustomed to on a day-to-day basis.

As for sex, procreation notwithstanding, it is still among the elements of transient pleasure. Recently, however, it has become the subject of a very interesting scientific study linking sex, money, and happiness.

Perhaps it's a little strange to think of relationships in financial terms, but a pair of scientists believed it was important enough to enlist the services of more than 50,000 people in the United States and England who agreed to be interviewed for their study. While love may not carry a price tag, David Blanchflower, PhD, of Dartmouth College, and Andrew Oswald, DPhil, of the University of Warwick in Britain, worked out the financial value of a good sex life.

"Sexual activity registers strongly positively in happiness equations," the study reports. "The more sex, the happier the person." (Hey, I could have told them that.) But the authors of the study went on to show that a good sex life has a financial value of about $55,000 a year. This is the amount of money it would take to bring people as much cheer as a regular sex life. (Just for the record, the scientists calculated that a loving marriage makes a person as happy as an extra $100,000 a year.) The study, titled "Money, Sex, and Happiness," was published in 2004 in the *Scandinavian Journal of Economics*.

The Burdens of Materialism

If you still are not sold on the idea that money doesn't buy happiness, let's go one step further. Let's see how much fun it can—*or cannot*—be to own everything you've always dreamed of.

Inflated Expectations

Let's play out everyone's fantasy. You're walking down the street by yourself on the way to the bus stop and notice a lottery ticket on the pavement. You pause. Should you pick it up? Oh, why not? *I'll just stick it in my handbag,* you think to yourself. *You never know . . .*

That night, you flip on the television, and—wonder of wonders—it turns out that the ticket you found is a *winner*! A *big* winner! Hurray for you! You can buy everything you ever wanted. And you *do*. You get the house, the sports car, and the Prada dresses. You're up in the stratosphere with joy!

Then, after a period of time, you drift quickly back to Earth. Something's wrong. You're rich, so why aren't you happier? Why are you going around humming that old Peggy Lee song, "Is That All There Is?"

We're mistaken when we believe that material things feed our souls. Sure, looking forward to buying that new convertible is exciting, but once you buy it, the thrill, while maybe not gone, is certainly diminished. It turns out that the expectations were far more exciting than the ownership. In other words, we think we're going to be happier than we end up being.

- Jennifer expected to be happy when her husband's promotion and raise came through, and for a while, she was. But his promotion meant he had to work longer hours, and in the end, he had less time for her and their two children. Result: four dissatisfied people.
- Andrea was the only one in her affluent circle of friends who didn't have a pool. Tired of always being a guest at other people's pools, she and her husband, Josh, decided to purchase their own so they could be the social center for their friends. Instead, they ended up sitting around their pool quite alone because, as they quickly learned, few people want to leave their own pool to go to someone else's.
- Lynne, a wealthy widow, fell in love with the owner of a local Greek diner in Scarsdale. She told her friends he was her "diamond in the rough." After a while, the charm of his "roughness," wore off, and Lynne decided it was time he had a makeover. She turned him into a "class act" by buying him Armani suits, broadening his horizons with travel, and quietly hiring a diction tutor to help him to lose his Brooklyn accent. He was a quick study and in time became so "classy" he no longer had any need for Lynne. His exit was short but not entirely sweet, and certainly not what she had expected.

When Too Much of a Good Thing
Is Too Much of a Good Thing

Ronnie came to my office several weeks ago looking like she really needed the vacation she had just started. "I know I'm going to sound spoiled, Dr. Baker," she said, "but I'm just so frustrated."

"What is it that's frustrating you?" I asked her. She appeared to be in her late thirties, and I knew from her registration forms that she was the wife of the CEO of a nationwide chain of retail stores based in San Francisco.

"My husband has just bought a vacation home for our family. In Barbados! Which is very nice. And I know I should be thrilled. I mean, it's great that he's doing so well, and we're really enjoying the fruits of his success. But deep down, we're a very simple family. We both came from middle-class backgrounds, and, well, we miss that."

"Then why not live the way you want?"

"Well, as he moved up the corporate ladder, we had to slowly change our lifestyle. You know, to be more in keeping with his position. It's kind of an unspoken obligation. But that meant leaving our comfortable split-level house in a very friendly neighborhood and moving to a bigger home on lots of land. We can't even *see* the house of our next-door neighbors, nor have we met them."

"Sounds like a bittersweet dilemma."

"It is, because now we have these big houses, and that means more taxes and more to care for and worry about. We need help, which means I have to find them and hire them and show them how we like things done. And when we're home, we're always bumping into them." She smiled at the image, but I knew she was serious. "Suddenly, there's no sense of privacy, no sense of family gathering, and I feel so responsible for all this *stuff*. What's happened is that these houses have started controlling *me*."

"Does your husband feel the same way?"

"He doesn't say so in so many words. But every so often he'll suggest we all get in the car and drive 40 minutes to our old neighborhood. We call our old friends and take the kids for pizza at the same place that used to be a big night out for us. And you know what? Sometimes we both wish we could go back in time. Even for just a little while."

Too Damn Many Choices

You saw in earlier chapters that approximately 50 percent of each person's happiness rests with either their set point (i.e., they are either born happy or not) or their circumstances (i.e., they've either got a lot going for them or they don't). But there is a third component: The impact we ourselves can make through our decisions and our actions.

In other words, much of our happiness is within our grasp—but only if we make the right choices.

Heaven knows, there are plenty of them. Americans are blessed and overwhelmed with choices. We are free to choose who our friends are, where we'll live, what jobs we'll work at, even how we'll look.

This freedom of choice is greatly enhanced by our increased wealth. In the past 40 years, the inflation-adjusted per capita income of Americans has more than doubled. And so have our choices. Have you tried to order a Coke lately? You need to choose among diet and regular Coke (with caffeine or caffeine-free), Lime Coke, Cherry Coke, Original Coke, Classic Coke, and more; in a liter bottle, 12-ounce bottle, or can. Want a pair of Levi's? There's relaxed fit and slim fit; boot cut and straight leg; low rise and high; sand washed, regular, and deep indigo. Remember when you could walk into a store, grab a pair of size 8 jeans off the rack, and be done? Those days are gone.

Here's the question: Are all these choices making us any happier, or have we hit upon yet another burden of materialism? It seems to me that increased choices can be problematic. For example, too many choices:

- Increase the burden of gathering information to make a wise decision.
- Increase the likelihood that we'll regret the decisions we make.
- Increase the feeling of missed opportunities. ("What if I looked a little harder? Maybe I'd find just what I want—at a better price!")
- Increase the chances that we'll blame ourselves when our choices turn out to be the wrong ones.

So now we have the money and the huge selection of things to purchase, and still we keep running ourselves ragged on that hedonic treadmill.

If you can slow down for just a second, ask yourself this.

If Money Won't Make Me Happy, Why Am I Working So Hard?

The answer is, because we all want to believe that there's a pot of gold at the end of the rainbow. And we just keep chasing it. America is a land of self-made success, and that means competing with (and beating) the other gal. You've got to be bigger, better, faster, and stronger. But is this really where we want to be? In the end, is it good for us? Or are we just caught up in it? For hundreds of thousands of years, we didn't have all this abundance, and to tell you the truth, I think people were richer (read, happier) then.

So does David Myers, PhD. In his landmark essay, *Does Economic Growth Improve Human Morale?* he wrote:

> Never has a culture experienced such physical comfort combined with such psychological misery. Never have we felt so free or had our prisons so overstuffed. Never have we been so sophisticated about pleasure or so likely to suffer broken relationships.

A poll by the University of Chicago's National Opinion Research Center led Dr. Myers to call America the doubly affluent society. He says, "In nearly 50 years, we have twice as many cars per person, microwave ovens, plasma TVs, home computers, and $200 billion a year spent in restaurants and bars—two and a half times our 1960 inflation-adjusted restaurant spending per person." And despite all this, we're not as happy as our parents and grandparents were.

And that's because *material goods are not what makes any of us really happy.*

Happy women know that possessions
are never enough to deliver happiness.

Happiness is more readily influenced by life events—marrying your college sweetheart, landing that dream job—and by possessing psychological characteristics such as optimism, a sense of belonging, and a feeling of self-esteem. Relationships are probably the most important barometer of happiness, particularly for women.

My grandmother was a teenager during World War I. She lived through the opulent era of the Roaring Twenties and watched the collapse of the stock market, followed by the Great Depression. No one had much of anything in those days, and her large, extended family had communal Sunday dinners, potluck style. The women worked together in the kitchen while the men smoked out on the porch. Or the men went fishing together while the women sat around with the children on their laps or at their breasts, sharing stories of their own grandparents. Even if it was by default, there was much togetherness, with an emphasis on relationships. And they were happy.

Fast-forward two generations. I may not be from Generation X or Generation Y or even the so-called Millennials, but like them, I am part of the mobile generation. Today no one lives in the same neighborhood for a lifetime—or even for decades. My wife and I don't know the Shultzes across the street because they just moved there yesterday. And why bother getting to know the Greens from down the block? In 3 years, they're going to move again—or we are. Even if they stayed, I might not *see* them very much because we could communicate through the convenience of e-mail instead of face to face.

My grandparents were happy people. They may not have had much, but they had enough—and they appreciated what they had.

The Only Tool You'll Need

If you keep in mind that happiness depends more on your state of mind than it does on your bank statement, you will understand that there can be only one tool to free you from the money trap: *Appreciate and focus on what you have and don't lament what you don't have.*

If you focus on what you *don't* have, you're going to be miserable. And that will happen again and again, because guaranteed, there will always be someone who has more than you do. If you look instead at what you do have, and I mean across the board, not simply the house and the car—if you look at your relationships and anything else that is meaningful to you, you cannot help but embrace and celebrate life for what it is.

Happy women know they can be rich for life if they focus more on what they have than on what they want.

Consider these two scenarios. Noontime: Rodeo Drive, Beverly Hills. Three young wanna-be starlets (WBS) have a date for lunch at the Ivy. Earlier in the week, WBS1 blew a week's salary at Ralph Lauren because the others have already seen her in her two good outfits, and to wear them again is unthinkable. WBS2 goes to lunch but doesn't eat anything because she's on a strict diet to lose those last 5 pounds (and because she probably scarfed down a few bagels for breakfast). Besides, she never eats anyway (in public.) WBS3 leaves her apartment early to take a bus across town. When she's several blocks away, she gets off the bus and walks down Rodeo Drive as though she's been shopping, so that her friends won't see that she can't afford a taxi.

The lunch lasts 48 minutes. WBS1 goes home to change because she might have to return the outfit she's wearing. WBS2, now feeling deprived and actually hungry, heads for the nearest Dunkin' Donuts. WBS3 heads for the bus stop, careful to duck into a store until the very last second so her friends won't see her getting on the bus when it comes.

Same time: Coral Gables, Florida. Three young women have a date for lunch at a local restaurant. One wears jeans, one is in shorts, and the third is dressed in the same skirt she wore the day before. The women order salads and begin to discuss the opening next month of the new arts center. One woman notes the beauty of the day. Another says how lucky she feels to be with her two best friends. The third announces that she's finally pregnant. Lunch lasts 2 hours. The women leave together, all remarking on the great choice of restaurant and how fortunate they feel to be friends.

The women in Coral Gables are happy because they know intuitively how to appreciate the good in what already exists, in what is both inside them and around them. In the end, *happy women know it's not the woman who dies with the most pairs of shoes who garners the prize; it's the one who has had the most fun dancing in them who is truly the winner.*

CHAPTER FOUR

When the Good You Do Doesn't Do You Any Good

*Women are traditionally trained
to place other's needs first . . .*

Tillie Olson

What could possibly be wrong with doing good? We want to please others, and we please ourselves when we do so. When we can do both at the same time, well, there's twice the pleasure.

Sounds easy, doesn't it? We've done it for as long as we can remember, from the time our first smiles drew approving oohs and ahhs from Mom or Dad. But the truth is, that thinking is a trap, pure and simple. The concept is based on the following logic: If I can make other people happy, then they will like me. If they like me, I must be good enough. If I'm good enough, they'll keep me around, I'll be safe and secure, and that's all I need to be happy.

The short take: The happier I can make others, the happier and therefore the safer I will be.

The only problem is, it doesn't work that way.

Make no mistake. There's nothing wrong with pleasing others—unless, of course, it becomes all-encompassing. If you give a portion of yourself here and a small piece there, a little energy here and a little time there, at some point, there's nothing left for you. True giving is a part of making any relationship work, but it's not the only part—particularly if you're doing all the giving and they're doing all the taking. Is that a recipe for a *balanced* relationship?

It's easy to get caught up in this state of affairs. Books have been written about it. So have myriad magazine and scientific journal articles. The patient in the starring role is known as a people pleaser, and the diagnosis, which was coined by Harriet Braiker, PhD, in her book of the same name, is "the disease to please." This malady starts with an earnest attempt to make someone else happy, but it can quickly become a pattern of behavior with far-reaching consequences. And it affects mostly women.

Why women? Don't *men* want to make others happy?

Of course they do, and some men are indeed people pleasers. But for starters, men generally don't try to please others by giving away pieces of themselves—or their power. Men please by giving away the stuff that having power affords. While men are very capable of giving out of pure altruism, they don't generally do it. Rather, they willingly give to curry favor, create obligations, demonstrate power, and court recognition for themselves. Men in general care less about whether someone likes them than they do about being recognized for something of importance. In other words, they are far less afflicted than women with "Sally Field syndrome," so named because upon being announced as the Academy Award winner for best actress, Field ran up to the lectern and blurted out, "You like me! You really like me!"

As mentioned earlier, women have evolved to be relationship driven, and they seek out social situations as opportunities to relate to others. They spend more time with the family than men do, which means they're on hand to do for others when the need arises.

⁌

In the days of our ancestors, almost every task required communication, coordination, and cooperation. In other words, a network of relationships supported every task. Evolution has virtually assured that women on the whole will be caregivers. The better early women were at these skills, the more value and status they realized within their families and their social circles.

In keeping with this concept, Shelley Taylor, PhD, a positive psychologist at the University of California, Los Angeles, has developed the theory that women's first type of stress response is not to fight or flee or freeze but to *tend and befriend*. In other words, in the face of an aggressor, a woman's first instinct is to try to make that aggressor into a friend. So, if the adversary is tough on her, she'll be nice, and if the adversary is tougher on her, she'll be nicer. If they're pushed hard enough, women will fight or flee if they feel the need to, but it's not their first line of defense. It's only in the end that biology takes over; women who are being assaulted will ultimately fight back or run away. This could be part of what motivates women to stay with abusive men. Instead of leaving them, they try to change them by pleasing them.

What Turns a Woman into a People Pleaser?

It can be any of a number of things, but the most notable is our old nemesis fear. *Fear of not being good enough.* The problem was, and still is, not so much what is expected of women but rather what would happen if they didn't meet those expectations. What if they just weren't "good enough"?

Fear of Abandonment

Fear of being abandoned prompts women to solicit the approval of others, even when it means putting the other person's needs or wants above their own. It's so powerful a fear that it often triggers a physiological reaction—the heart rate speeds up—at the very thought of banishment. In prehistoric times, perhaps the most fearsome punishment that could be meted out was to be sent away from the family, the clan, the village, the tribe, or the religious sect, all of which were quite literally life-giving. In most cases, exile was tantamount to a slow and agonizing death, if not always physically, then certainly emotionally.

Modern women need to be included, just as their female forebears did (men do, too, but they just don't recognize it or express it in the same clear, strong way). Women are all about relationships; they know and understand that they need them. Fear of abandonment is another reason that so many women remain in abusive situations. For them, the idea of being alone is more frightening than the possibility of more abuse.

Fear of Being Excluded

This fear underpins the need to be liked by everyone, to remain on the "A" party list, to be invited to the important meeting, or to be let in on the latest gossip. Who doesn't want to be the prom queen?

Several years ago, I was a guest on a radio phone-in show in Atlanta. A woman with a youthful voice, who identified herself as Samantha, called in complaining, "I've always put myself out for my friends and family, and now they're beginning to take advantage of my good nature. You know what, Doctor? I don't want to do it anymore."

"Can you give me an example of what you're referring to?" I asked.

"Well, sure. About a year ago, I decided to leave my job to become a fulltime mom. It only took a few weeks for my neighbors to realize I was home most of the time, and all of a sudden I was the go-to mom for every kid on the block. It's gotten way out of hand. 'Can you pick up my son?' 'Can you let my dog out?' 'Can you let the electrician in?' Along with my own kids, I'm shuttling everyone else's kids all over the place, too. I don't mind in an emergency, but it's happening more and more, and frankly, I feel taken advantage of. Half of them don't even call to say thank you."

"If this were the best of all possible worlds," I said, "what would you *like* to do?"

"What would I like to do? I'd like to be able to sit at home and enjoy my children and not dread the phone when it rings."

She didn't use these words, but I think what she really wanted to know was *How do I get myself out of this bind without everyone hating me?* I asked her this: "Samantha, are you an honest person? Do you value honesty?"

"Sure."

"I'm not so sure," I said. "If you're really honest, you have to act like the person you think you are, which, as I see it, gives you two choices. You either have to give without a whole lot of expectation of anything coming back, or you need to recognize that maybe you're not the person you want people to think you are. In which case, you have to deal with the consequences."

"What consequences?"

"Well, some of these people may not like you as much." There was a silence, and I assumed she was mulling over my comment. But the host of the show broke in and thanked her for her call, then ran a 2-minute commercial, and we were on to the next person. My guess is she had probably heard all she wanted to hear anyway.

I did understand where she was coming from, though. Who doesn't want to be liked? Who doesn't want to belong? These feelings hark back to our days in elementary school. I remember routinely playing softball with my friends even though I *hated* softball. Heaven forbid if I was the last kid chosen for the team. It was a fate worse than death for a 9-year-old, and as you know, no matter how old we are, we still remember what it feels like to be the last one chosen. Part of the horrible ritual included making the last one picked know, in no uncertain terms, that they really weren't wanted on a ball field or anywhere else. It's all the same—and a fate we'd all like to avoid.

Fear of Anger and Confrontation

This particular fear leads a woman to say yes when she means no. It also keeps her from asking for what she really wants because she's afraid of upsetting her partner, boss, friend, child, or even a stranger. Why? Because confrontation suggests there's going to be a winner and a loser, and she may very well lose, so rather than fight, she backs off. The concept is a lot like the theory of learned helplessness developed by Martin Seligman, PhD, which you read about in Chapter 1. You've been burned so many times that you'd rather give in than fight. After a while, it becomes a habit, and you no longer even consider the options. You just give in.

Now if you're a guy like Donald Trump, for instance, you don't mind confrontation. In fact, you probably even enjoy it because in the past, you've come out on top most of the time. When I go to buy a new car, I love to do my homework and then dicker and play with the salesperson: "Oh, come on, throw in the nickel-plated lug nuts for free. And hey, while you're at it, why not give me a free undercoating, too?"

My wife, on the other hand, hates any kind of haggling. If she can get close to a fair price for the car, she writes a check on the spot and she's out of there. Sure, the salesman likes her. Why wouldn't he? He's made a very nice commission with very little hassle. In effect, my wife has pleased herself by pleasing a car salesman.

Well, it's fine to want to be liked and to want to avoid conflict, but remember, it's not fine when it costs you dearly. Every time you say yes when you want to say no, it takes a bite out of your self-esteem because you have actually determined that your desires are secondary to someone else's. Keep doing that, and eventually there is no self-esteem left.

Janet's Story

Janet came to my office not too long ago, all smiles. A stunning woman who looked to be in her late fifties, she was a book editor for one of the larger Boston publishers. She appeared to be the picture of good health and great energy—the kind of woman Canyon Ranch showcases in its ads.

"How is life treating you?" I asked her after she settled herself on the sofa.

"Life is good, Dr. Baker. Life is really good."

"That's great!" I said, and meant it. "Why don't we discuss some of the good things and let's see if we can keep that feeling going, or even make it just the slightest bit better."

"Well," she paused, glancing upward at the ceiling, "there actually *is* one small situation that just happened. Maybe you can give me some advice. I know it's going to come up again."

I agreed to offer the best advice I knew.

"My son and his family live in New York, and every few months, I travel from Boston to see them and to spend time with my friends. But it seems every time I plan to go, if I so much as mention it to my son, I can always count on being enlisted by my daughter-in-law to take their preschooler somewhere. The scenario is always the same: She'll call and say, 'Don't you want to spend time with your *granddaughter*?' And of course, I do. But on *my* schedule, at least some of the time. Not hers."

"Can you give me an example?"

"Okay. This happened a few weeks ago. I planned to visit the city for two days—Wednesday and Thursday. I had made a lunch date with an old friend for Wednesday. Of course, at some point I planned to see the grandchildren, so a few days before I left, I called my son to tell him I was coming. Three hours later—no surprise—my phone rang; it was Stacy. 'I heard you're coming in next week. You can take Amanda to her dance lesson on Wednesday. Then lunch. She'd love that!' Not 'Can you?' but 'You can.' "

"Wednesday was when you planned to have lunch with your friend," I said. "Did you tell her?"

"No."

"Why not?

"I don't know. I just switched my date. So that morning, I picked up Mandy and took her to dancing school. And in truth, I was actually looking forward to watching her spin around in her little leotard. But no sooner did we get inside the school than the teacher whisked all the children away and took them to another room."

"Could you at least see her through a window?"

"No. That's the point. They closed the door. That left me waiting in this windowless anteroom for an hour with nothing to read and no class to observe. I'd been instructed not to leave in case Mandy needed me. It was awful."

She let out a growl, remembering another detail. "Oh, and listen to this. While I was there, Stacy called to tell me she forgot she had made a play date for Mandy, so would I just drop her off at her friend's directly after school? Then I was free to go."

"To which you replied . . . ?"

"What could I say? She's my daughter-in-law. I said, 'Fine.' But I was furious."

"I'm curious. Why didn't you tell her you had planned to take Amanda out for lunch?"

"Who knows?" she shrugged. "Maybe I didn't want to rock the boat. Anyway, what got me the most wasn't that she *treated* me like a nanny but rather that I *let* her." The truth was, her daughter-in-law controlled one of the most powerful motivators in Janet's life, her granddaughter.

"And how would you have wanted her to treat you?"

"Like a grandmother. Like the grandmother of her children."

"But you behaved like . . ."

"I know. Like a nanny."

"Hmm. It seems to me that if you want to be treated like a grandmother, you have to *act* like one. What you did was, you gave your power away to your daughter-in-law. Now it's up to you to take it back."

"That," she said with hint of a smile, "is easier said than done."

"Let me ask you a question. How would your work life be if you ran it the same way you are allowing your personal life to be run? I know *my* business would be in chaos. What happens if you work with your daughter-in-law to find a win/win outcome essentially the way you would with one of your authors?

"You need to believe that what you bring to your daughter-in-law's life and to your grandchild's is every bit as valuable as what they bring to yours. And until you make up your mind that that's the way it is, you will forever be dealing from a one-down position."

Operating from a one-down position is a slippery slope in that it reinforces that feeling of not being enough. You don't feel as if you're strong enough to hold your own, hence the ease with which you give in to someone else. I then told Janet a story that contains one of my favorite metaphors: In India, when they raise an elephant to work in the lumber industry, they begin training the animal when he's a newborn calf. They put a manacle on his leg, and it's attached to a little chain, which is held fast by a stake in the ground. The baby animal walks out, and when he reaches the end of his tether, he is forced to stop.

As the elephant grows, they change the manacle's size to accommodate his growing leg. Meanwhile, the elephant's strength grows, too, but he still walks to the end of the chain and then stops. By the time that elephant is an adult, he has many times the strength needed to break that chain, but—as with Dr. Seligman's dogs—because he's been defeated so many times, he no longer tries. Here's where the message for us adult humans comes in: Take advantage of being full-grown and use your strength to break those chains if you want to break them.

What Janet did by saying yes when she wanted to say no was violate her own values. As a result, she found herself at odds with a difficult foe—herself. She didn't have an unlimited amount of energy or time, and yet she let someone else dictate how she used the time and energy she did have.

Here was a highly successful executive, well respected in publishing—a field that on a good day is not for the faint of heart—and she hesitated to stand up to her daughter-in-law. Why?

Because she was afraid to. When you are living in fear of something or someone, when you're dealing with negative emotions, your vision narrows, and you lose a broader perspective on the world. In situations like this, people can't see anything but that which they fear. If Janet had denied her daughter-in-law's request, Stacy might have stamped her feet and given Janet the silent treatment for a while, but she would have gotten over it.

I asked Janet to try to express specifically what scared her. "It's simple," she told me. "Have you ever heard of the golden rule? *He who has the gold makes the rules.* My daughter-in-law is the mother of my grandchild. As far as I'm concerned, she holds the gold."

This scenario plays out all over the world at every level of society, and it can involve a daughter-in-law or just as easily a child who wants to be driven to a friend's house a half hour away right before you're expecting 25 guests for dinner.

Can you see how this is a very subtle trap? You think you're pleasing someone by doing what they want at the expense of what you want, but I can tell you, you're not doing anyone any good. Pleasing others to the detriment of pleasing yourself doesn't stop with a single exchange. Eventually, as we saw in both of the above examples, people come to expect as the norm what you did as an exception. It becomes a self-reinforcing and self-fulfilling expectation, and thus a vicious cycle is set in motion.

Beyond the Fear

Not everyone becomes a people pleaser out of fear. There are other reasons women fall into this trap, such as these.

- **Your mother set the pattern by being a self-sacrificer.** When I think of how mothers set examples for their children, I can't help thinking about the pot roast story. One day, a child observed her mother cutting a pot roast in two in preparation for cooking. "Why do you cut the meat into two pieces?" the child asked innocently. The mother responded, "Because that's the way my mother did it." The child, being bright and precocious, remembered her mother's explanation, and the next time she visited her grandmother, she put the same question to her. The reply was the same: "Because my mother did it that way, and I learned from her." Later the great-grandmother came by the house, and the child (not one to let things go easily!) posed the question yet again. Great-grandmother explained that when she was a young wife and mother, she didn't possess a pan large enough to hold a whole pot roast, so she had to cut the meat into two smaller pieces to fit it all into the two smaller pans she did own. Such is the power of mothers. We rarely question and often imitate.
- **Doing for others can be seductive.** This is particularly true when you begin to feel "one up" on the person you're pleasing. It's in part a

corollary to the one-down feeling, but in this case, you come out way ahead. (Here I feel compelled to recall the actions of Don Corleone in *The Godfather*. He was constantly doing favors, and it seemed the whole world "owed him.")

- **Doing good feels good physically and literally elevates your mood.** Ever felt or heard of a "runner's high"? That high comes from the release of endorphins into the bloodstream, triggered by vigorous exercise. Some people get addicted to exercise because they build up a tolerance to the endorphins. Over time, they need more and more endorphins to feel the same high, and they exercise until they get it. You can create the same feelings (since your body releases the very same neurotransmitters) by doing something good for someone— and it can become equally addictive.

- **Some people give love conditionally.** Sometimes parents, friends, and spouses express love only when you comply with their wishes, sending the message that you are lovable only if you please them.

The 1,000-Pound Barbell

Human beings exhibit amazing plasticity, but they can be stretched or can stretch themselves to the breaking point. Without much effort, the need to please creeps up on you. Consider this: If you went to the gym and someone pointed to a 1,000-pound barbell and told you to lift it, you couldn't. If you even tried, you'd surely end up hurting yourself in all sorts of ways. But women will try to lift that barbell! They start with a 5-pound weight and add just a few ounces at a time. Over time, the weight becomes more than they can handle, but until they have actually hurt themselves, they don't stop. They can't see exactly where that breaking point is.

Hillel Was Right

Rabbi Hillel was a Talmudic scholar whose moral and legal decisions remain the cornerstone of Jewish tradition. Two thousand years ago, Hillel put forward three prescient questions that are just as relevant today as they were back then.

1. If I am not for myself, who will be for me?
2. If I am not for others, what am I?
3. If not now, when?

Question #1: If I Am Not for Myself, Who Will Be for Me?

This question is about self-interest. When people first hear it, they wonder, *Why would I want to be that way? It's so selfish.* But it's not. There is a huge difference between self-interest and selfishness. Acting in your own self-interest means doing things only you can do for yourself. And if you don't do those things, you will be a lesser being for it. It resonates with Chapter 6, where we illustrated how the quality of your life is greatly determined by the overall quality of your relationships, *starting with the one you have with yourself.*

Think about it this way. Much as you might want to, you can't save a drowning person if you don't know how to swim.

Happy women know that if you want to take care of others, you must first—or simultaneously—take care of yourself.

Philosopher Tom Norris, PhD, points out in his book *If Aristotle Ran General Motors* that there are some things only you can do for yourself. You can't delegate them, you can't buy them, and you can't ignore them without consequence. For example, nobody can exercise for you, nobody can choose the food you put in your body, and nobody can tell you what to think or how to spend your time.

It's not only these things that are important, however. Like time and money, energy, emotion, and physical stamina are finite resources that can be overdrawn, leaving you empty and depleted. You must also care for your psyche and your soul, and if you do those things, if you take proper care of yourself, the self you bring to the table with your partner, children, friends, and employees will be a far better self. If you neglect that self, you're not only doing others in your close circles a disservice, you're doing yourself a disservice as well.

How to Have a Relationship with Yourself

First, ask yourself these questions.

- What have I done to take care of my body today?
- What have I done to take care of my mind today?
- What have I done to take care of my spirit today?

I'm not speaking hypothetically or even generally, but very specifically. What observable, measurable actions have you taken? Here are a few suggestions to get you started, but you can implement any of your own ideas that work for you.

- **To care for your body, make good decisions about diet and exercise.** Neither of these is my area of expertise, but I'm certain that you've heard the speech from your physician. If you haven't, that's the first place to start. As to which diet and exercise plan is right for you, there's one correct answer: The one that you will do consistently. Recognizing that you're not the Energizer Bunny and that you're a human being with finite resources that need periodic replenishing is key to caring for yourself. Take time off for a massage, a manicure, and a walk in the woods with a friend. Do something fun for yourself, particularly if you spend most of your time caring for others.

• **To take care of your mind, stimulate, stimulate, stimulate.** The brain is plastic, which means it's continually growing, long into adulthood. To keep it in top shape, take an interest in something separate from your everyday responsibilities. Talk to other adults whom you find energizing. Go to lectures, watch documentaries, and learn something new every day, even if it's only a new word. Life will be more interesting, and so will you.

• **To take care of your spirit, learn what you need to find peace.** Do you need to be touched? Do you need to be in a quiet, nurturing place, like a synagogue, church, gallery, or garden? Some people nurture their spirits by picking up the telephone and talking to the people they love. Others use journaling, counting their blessings, or even pulling out an album and spending an hour with photos of people and places they love.

Women often comment, "I'm so busy taking care of my kids *and* my parents, how can I possibly carve out an hour for myself?" I say, how can you *not*? God forbid, but if you had a heart attack, who would take care of your parents? Well, call that person. Here's the truth: You have the same amount of time everyone else has, so it's never really about time; it's about priorities.

If you add up all these small things, they probably amount to a little more than an hour a day you'll need for yourself. You exercise for 30 to 40 minutes, eat as you would anyway, and then read an article you've been meaning to get to. Or sit in your garden, listen to music, or pick up the phone and call that old friend. It's not hard—and you don't have to do it all at the same time. You don't have to give 60 minutes of every hour to your newborn quintuplets. You can still take 5 of them for yourself.

Question #2: If I Am Only for Myself, What Am I?

As much as the first question proffers self-interest, that's how much the second cautions against selfishness. Hillel understood that after you take care of yourself, there is a whole world of other people out there to be considered. And while self-interest is about taking care of yourself in ways only you can do, selfishness is all about self-absorption.

Selfish people are emotional black holes who can and often do suck the life out of those around them. Five words sum them up: the highest of high maintenance. They are easy to spot, though, because their speech is overloaded with personal pronouns, namely *I, me,* and *mine.* J. K. Rowling captured this type of character beautifully in the Harry Potter series with her creatures, the dementors.

These are the very people who attract the self-sacrificers—the people pleasers. These two get along very well because in a very unhealthy way, one is yin to the other's yang. You give—I take. This is a direct route to martyrdom for the giver, and it works out equally well for the one on the taking end.

But where is the *balance* in this relationship?

Question #3: If Not Now, When?

We tend to operate on a day-to-day basis as if we have forever. You know the litany. You'll get around to taking care of yourself tomorrow, next week, next month. But life has a way of reminding us from time to time that all we really have is this moment. A number of years ago, my wife and I went looking at homes one Sunday afternoon. On one of these forays, we met a lovely woman, a real estate agent. We signed the book agents use to build a database and then went on our way. From then on, this lady kept in contact with us, and once a year we received a holiday card with some personal sentiment expressed.

Several years later, when we decided to make a move, we called her and made an appointment for the following week. She couldn't meet us earlier, she said, because she needed to go out of town that weekend to attend her daughter's wedding. On the Sunday preceding our meeting, I was reading the local newspaper and came across a story that shocked me to the core. The story reported this woman's murder the day before, the very day she was to fly to be with her daughter for her wedding. I'll spare you the gory details; suffice it to say that it demonstrates very clearly what Hillel was saying: We have now and *only* now.

Happy women understand that today is all we can be
sure of, and they know how to make the most of it.

Rabbi Hillel was obviously an extremely wise man, for he well understood that happiness is often a function of giving and taking and that to do too much of one without the other leads to an imbalanced life of either martyrdom or self-absorbed gluttony.

Here's a tool to make sure you get it right: Find the balance that works for you, and be aware that this balance will change over your lifetime, depending on your circumstances. Every day, ask yourself: *Have I answered Hillel's questions to my real satisfaction today?* If you generally get a yes back, then study what you are doing right and build on it. If you are getting more no answers, then study what you're doing on those days that come as close to yes as possible and dedicate yourself to doing more of that.

When the Person You're Pleasing Is Connected to You

Over the years, I have spent much time in my office with the proverbial "soccer moms," who run their kids from soccer to violin lessons to religious classes. I have listened with great interest to the ways in which an adult's life—including her social life—seems to now revolve around the children. Vacations include the children; dinner parties include the children. And the childrearing tactics have changed, too. From my limited vantage point, it appears that today's parents hate to say no to their children. This of course sets the stage for difficulty later because the world will say no many times regardless of one's station in life, and it's always a good idea to have the capacity to deal effectively with it when it happens.

Don't get me wrong; I'm not passing judgment here. Not at all. I've raised my own kids, certainly not without error, but my concern is that these mothers are modeling self-sacrifice. They're setting a model for their little girls that *this is what mommies do.* Mommies give to everybody else to the point of exhaustion and beyond. Mommies never take care of themselves first.

This is not a good message. In fact, it's a very confusing one because at some point, when the girl you're doing everything for grows up and has her own daughter, your daughter is sure to get caught in the middle. She has always expected everything to be done for her, but the only model she has for how to be a mother is someone who took self-sacrificing to new heights: a self-sacrificer. Suddenly she's expected to do for everyone else. How can she possibly enjoy motherhood?

Many mothers—the working ones in particular—come to me complaining of exhaustion. I counseled a mother of three recently who told me she played the role of chauffeur, homework supervisor, personal shopper, cheerleader, pastry chef, and relationship counselor. She had no time for herself. "Why did I bother to go to graduate school?" she wailed.

I asked her to reverse the roles. I said, "How would you like it if your daughter never went outside to play? How would you like your child to go weeks without talking to a friend because she's so busy with other things?"

It was no surprise to hear her say, "I wouldn't like it."

"Well," I said, "this is the model you're putting in front of your children."

So, if you're going with your pedal to the metal, all stops pulled out and with nothing coming in, ask yourself if it's worth it. Is it the life you want and one you'd be happy to see your kids living when they have children of their own?

The Magic Word (Hint: It's Not *Please*)

Remember Samantha, the woman I spoke to on the radio show? She felt trapped and taken advantage of by her neighbors and friends. If our conversation hadn't been cut off, if we'd had a little more time, here's the tool I would have suggested she employ—and this will work just as well for you if you worry about being a people pleaser: *Just stop saying yes every time you're asked.*

Okay, let's give Nancy Reagan her due. You, too, can "just say no!"

Oh, I know, it's easier said than done. But you can do it. You may need to practice, and even more important, you'll need to be on your guard at the beginning because the word *yes* has a way of slipping out before we even know it's gone.

If you're a happy person who smiles a lot, you'll notice that the word *yes* comes with a smile. Try it. Now try saying no with a smile. It doesn't work. And that is one of the reasons it's so hard to say no—particularly if you want to please all of the people all of the time.

The Power of *No*

Have you ever been in the company of a toddler who has just learned the power of the word *no*? As children hatch into independence, it becomes their favorite word. Saying no establishes individuality between self and not self. It's a healthy way for a toddler to start breaking away from Mother.

No is the most powerful word in the English language. Saying no is a potential lifesaver. It's about respecting yourself—your needs, your values, your time, and your energy.

This isn't about saying no to other people as much as it is about saying yes to yourself. In my book, the saying "time is money" is wrong. Time is life. When I give it away, I give away heartbeats. If I go to dinner with someone for 3 hours, I give away 13,000 heartbeats. Is it going to be worth it? Am I going to leave the restaurant saying that it was nice, the wine was great, the conversation was interesting? Or am I going walk out and say, "Man, I should have been home, preparing for those meetings tomorrow. Now I'm going to be up all night, and I'm tired already." That's going to war with yourself.

Thus, an important tool for fighting your way out of this trap is honesty. If you don't want to go to dinner with a friend, say so. You might say, for example, "I really hope you understand when I say no that it's not about you, it's about taking care of me. It's about giving myself a quiet evening at home when I desperately need it. About soaking in the tub with a good book and trying to unwind. It's about listening to some music that I bought months ago and haven't had 5 minutes to listen to yet." You will be amazed at how doing something so simple puts you in alignment with yourself. Living in a way that is aligned with your values is tremendously enhancing.

Here are some more workable tools to help you better manage your tendency to please others by sacrificing yourself.

* Before responding to someone's request, always buy yourself some time to weigh the consequences of your decision by saying, "I need to think about it first. I'll get back to you," or "let me check my schedule

and call you back." That's a reasonable response. It buys you time to decide what you want to do, and you can get back to the person after you have chosen to accept or established a good excuse to refuse.

• Practice phrases with the word *no* in them just to get comfortable with how it feels to say it. Do it when you're alone, then start with small steps and gradually work your way up to more difficult situations, like saying no to your mother (remember, you can always change your mind).

• Discover what gives you pleasure and do it. Indulge yourself. Give yourself permission to watch a favorite show, even if the dishes are piled in the sink and there's laundry to be done. Enjoy what you enjoy for the sake of doing it for yourself.

• Do a reality check of your feelings when you're in situations where you're apt to fall back into people-pleasing mode, such as Janet did with her daughter-in-law. Does your daughter-in-law (like Janet's) assume you're going to be available to help whenever she needs it? It's not *always* possible to lend a hand. Work toward saying what's on your mind, even if it means taking a risk. The first time is always the most difficult.

When Saying No Isn't an Option

There are some cases where ethics and morality compel a yes. There are difficult situations in life that all of us must step up to. A child becomes ill, parents get older, a sister develops breast cancer. These are challenging situations that require extraordinary effort to cope with. We don't invite these circumstances; they find us. That's life.

When elderly parents fall ill and become incapacitated, if there are both female and male children, most often it is a daughter who ends up with the lion's share of caregiving. Likewise, when the parents of the husband fall ill, it's often the wife (daughter-in-law) who takes on the responsibility of caretaking. That's because in this and most other societies, a woman's identity and worth are so strongly tied to her ability to care for others.

When you have no choice but to be a caretaker, it's essential to take equal care of yourself and the person who needs it. The key is to make choices that serve you well. This is where the 60-minute principle can come in handy.

This principle says there are 60 minutes in every hour, and you need to look at the quality of your choices and prioritize the positive ones. If for 30 minutes out of that hour those choices are serving you well, and for 30 minutes they're working against you, instead of trying to reduce the time that's working against you, work at increasing the time you spend on the things that are working *for* you. The point is, there are still only 60 minutes in that hour, so you crowd out the bad things and focus on the good—on what works for you in life.

Happy women know that downtime is not a luxury;
it is essential to well-being.

Not long ago, we had a guest at the ranch whose brothers had bought her a week's stay. "They decided I needed a break," she said. It turned out that this woman was a single parent caring for her autistic son, and although she never complained to them about it, her older siblings decided this would be great for her. We talked about the stress she was under, and she asked me how she might better care for herself. We discussed the ideas outlined in this chapter, but I wanted something more for her—something special she could do with her son. It was summer, and I thought about gardening. She lived in an apartment in Brooklyn with no yard, but we decided that she could still have window boxes full of flowers. Taking care of a single flower is still gardening.

Several weeks after she left the ranch, I received a letter. She wrote about the joys of putting her hands in the earth. It gave her energy, she said "to grow something beautiful . . ." She enclosed a photograph of herself and her son smiling next to their "garden," which was nothing more than a window box filled with white petunias and a single red geranium. But clearly the mother, son, and flowers were all in full bloom. This was a woman who had learned how to say yes to herself.

Happiness is not found in pleasing others at the expense of self. It is not doing what others think you should do. Happiness comes when you do what pleases you for the sake of pleasing yourself. Think about this for a moment: No one could quibble that Mother Teresa was one of the most altruistic people of the 20th century. She didn't *have* to do what she was doing. She did it because it pleased her. From my observation, she found profound personal pleasure in caring for others and serving God.

As benevolent and altruistic and saintly as Mother Teresa was, she said no to certain things—things that she felt violated people's privacy or dignity. When Anne Ryder, a television reporter we interviewed, asked to visit her institution, Mother Teresa initially turned her down. But Ryder persevered, and when Mother Teresa recognized that her intentions were purely selfless, she ultimately agreed to the visit as well as an interview.

Understanding the Difference between Being Civil, Being Nice, and Pleasing

Civility is a standard of conduct that allows you to be at your constructive best. It really doesn't matter if you are dealing with someone who is deeply appreciative of you and your efforts or someone who is so insatiable that no matter what you do, it will never be enough. Civility will always ensure that you keep and possibly enhance your self-respect. It is driven by your values and considers the question of how all parties, including yourself, may be best served while at the same time understanding that sometimes it isn't possible to satisfy everyone. Civility guarantees that your conduct is considerate and decent but not necessarily compliant with others' wishes and/or demands.

Being nice is generally a desirable trait, except for when it's a veil for subordination and submission. In this rough-and-tumble world, it is at times unfortunately seen as a weakness. I once met a runner-up from Donald Trump's TV show, *The Apprentice*. While she had all the attributes to be very successful in business—and was one of the final two left standing—she was the last one fired. Trump fired her because he believed she was "too nice." Understand that nice people generally view and treat others with kindness and respect, but they also do the same for themselves, so they aren't prone to say yes and to please at any and all cost. Pleasing is generally a good thing as long as it is genuine and meaningful and leads to satisfaction, not martyrdom.

When you're doing something good for someone—pleasing them, if you will—and that something doesn't feel right or good, it's a signal to you to closely examine your position and conduct before proceeding further.

In recent years, the word *boundaries* has come into vogue. I've always had difficulty with this word because it smacks a little of psychobabble, and I'm one psychologist who tries to stay as far away as I can from that jargon. Humans have enough challenges when it comes to making healthy connections; we don't need to focus on the things that separate us. There is a word that has been around much longer, and to me it is far more powerful: *respect*. At the end of the day, can you say your choices helped you maintain or even improve your self-respect? And your respect for others?

If you can answer yes, you can be confident that the disease to please will probably never strike you. If you can't, then work on some of the tools in this chapter, and you will see a measurable difference. I guarantee it.

CHAPTER FIVE

The Revenge Rut

Never does the human soul appear so strong as when it foregoes revenge and dares to forgive an injury.

Edwin Hubbel Chapin

She never saw it coming. On a city street in Las Vegas, two cars collided head on. One driver walked away. In the other car lay the limp body of off-duty corrections officer Suzanne Mikols, her head sandwiched at a disturbing angle between the airbag and the seat of her car.

When she awoke from her coma in the intensive care unit 2 weeks later, she learned that the driver of the other car—an uninsured methamphetamine addict just days out of prison—had been heading north. At the tail end of a 36-hour bender, he had fallen asleep at the wheel and drifted into the southbound lane. Her doctors told her that she'd suffered a severe injury to her brain and might never quite return to her former self; that years of rehabilitation lay ahead of her; and that perhaps, if she was very lucky, she could one day return to her position at the Las Vegas Detention Center—but she shouldn't count on it.

Yet, in an essay she later wrote about the accident, she called it:

> A tragic story that transformed misfortune into a glorious
> celebration! This was something that could have broken my

heart as well as my head. But it didn't. Instead, I lived to experience the joy of true friendship and the spiritual uplifting of my soul! I'm so grateful for the chance to have had this major struggle that rocked my world . . .

At about the same time Mikols was being rushed into the emergency room, this exchange between a mother and daughter was taking place during lunch in the Canyon Ranch dining room.

"I swear to God, if I had a rifle, I'd blast the SOB wide open."

"Mom, stop. It's 22 years since Daddy left."

"I don't care. I still want to kill that snake. But slowly. I want him to suffer."

"Mom. We've been over this a million times. Besides, he's been dead for 4 years."

"What does *that* have to do with anything?"

These two examples illuminate the difference between a life being lived and a life being squandered, between shaping your own future and being so entrenched in revenge that you can't see past it. Let's take a look at how these women came to these two very different places.

What Is Revenge?

Revenge is a plan to punish or get even with someone in retaliation for the harm they caused you. It's fine to entertain thoughts of revenge, and it can even be satisfying, but when the fantasies go on and on, they become a trap. That trap is almost guaranteed to harm you more than it harms the person you're plotting against. You may think you're getting even, but think about this while you're at it: Every minute taken up in this fruitless pursuit (you're not *really* going to pull the trigger) is a minute of your life you've thrown away.

Despite the preponderance of Western movies in which a wronged man sets out to exact revenge on another, vengeance is more a woman's issue than a man's.

One reason women are more likely than men to fall into the revenge rut is simply because of the ways in which they have been socialized. I was a proctor in a college dormitory for a few years. If two of the guys in the dorm had an argument, they'd shout it out or go down to the parking lot and get physical. In either case, when it was over, it was over. Buddies again, they'd head to the local watering hole and buy each other a beer.

The girls, however, were different. After a disagreement, most would gossip about and pick at each other, sometimes for weeks. Although both males and females are *biologically* disposed to fight, flee, or freeze in the face of perceived danger, women are not *socially* disposed to those responses. Let's say a girl is the subject of a malicious and unfounded rumor that has wrecked her social life. Let's also assume she knows who started said rumor. Will she go up and punch the rumormonger in the face? I doubt it. Will she run away at the sight of her enemy? No to that suggestion, too. This leaves only a few other options: internalizing the anger, railing against something safer, or staying up nights plotting revenge.

Here's where it gets you both ways: A multitude of studies make connections between suppressed anger and increased vulnerability to illness. Research from a long-term study done at the University of Michigan suggests that "chronic anger may be more damaging to women than to men" because of suppression. This is reinforced by a study done in Sweden that showed women who were socially isolated and unable to discuss angry feelings may have a greater risk of heart disease. Interestingly, the same report also suggested that women who vent their anger were generally more pessimistic, lacked social support, sensed limited control over their lives, and had greater health problems. So are you damned if you do, and damned if you don't? The answer is no. Not if you find a *constructive way* to express your anger. Later in this chapter, you will meet women who have learned ways to do just that. When a woman acts on the impulse for revenge, the outcome can get pretty violent, particularly when a man is on the receiving end. That makes sense when you think about it because if a woman doesn't make her point on her first effort, she may not get a second chance.

I recall reading about several women who played out their revenge in ways that were irresistible to the media; their names quickly became household words. Aileen Wuornos's story was the basis of the movie *Monster,* which brought Charlize Theron an Academy Award. Wuornos claimed to have been sexually abused as a young woman. In retaliation, this self-professed vigilante drove the roads of south Florida, picked up men with the promise of a good time, and then took them into the woods and exacted her revenge with a pistol. I'm not sure of the count (it was somewhere around seven), but quite a few men paid with their lives for the sins of someone they never knew.

Lorena Bobbitt's husband made the mistake of cheating on her. Planning the ultimate female revenge, Bobbitt waited until her husband was asleep, pulled a kitchen knife from the drawer, and whacked off his penis. If nothing else, she sent an undeniable message to him (and I'm certain to many other men across the country). I don't think he'll ever cheat on anyone again (at least not in the usual way).

Finally, there is Amy Fisher, the "Long Island Lolita." Fisher walked up the front steps of the home of her lover, Joey Buttafuocco, and rang the bell. When Buttafuocco's wife came to the door, Fisher shot her point blank in the face. In her mind, the wife stood in the way of happily ever after for her and Buttafuocco.

Each of these women was gifted for her efforts with years of confinement (Bobbitt was sent to a psychiatric hospital, Fisher and Wuornos served jail time, and Wuornos was ultimately executed).

On the other end of the spectrum are incredibly resilient women—women like Suzanne Mikols—who chose to grow from traumatic experiences rather than seek revenge. Some of these women, too, have had their 15 minutes of fame. One of the best known in recent years is a woman who clearly showed the world what courage is all about. For a decade, she was known only as the Central Park jogger.

On the evening of April 19, 1989, 28-year-old Trisha Meili, an investment banker at Salomon Brothers, set out alone on her usual after-work run in Central Park. She knew she was taking a risk running alone in the evening, but she truly believed no one would ever harm her. And she was right, at least until that particular evening. It was well after dusk when somewhere at the north end of the park, Meili was assaulted, pulled into some thick bushes, tied up, raped, beaten, and left for dead. The EMTs who arrived to take her to the hospital didn't think she'd get there alive.

What they—or the assailant, for that matter—didn't know was how deeply ingrained and indomitable was the positive spirit of this self-empowered woman.

After almost 2 weeks in a coma, Meili woke to find herself unable to walk, talk, read, or dress herself. But in keeping with who she is, she pushed herself through an accelerated rehabilitation program and eventually returned to her old job. She found that things weren't the same, however. She was less interested now in putting deals together and more concerned with helping people—people like herself who had been through great trauma or were struggling to live their lives with permanent disabilities.

Meili left the job she once loved and found a calling that she loves even more. She is now a motivational speaker and volunteer who talks to large and small groups about her life and her healing. She will never again be the person she was before the attack, but despite her physical and mental limitations, her life has a purpose, which she finds to be immensely rewarding.

Despite, or more likely because of, her trauma and the challenges and opportunities it created, Trisha Meili is a happy woman.

Revenge Can Drag You Down

Being trapped in the revenge rut is like being in a car that's stuck in the mud after a 4-day rain. The wheels are spinning, but you're not getting anywhere. And the longer the wheels spin, the deeper the rut.

This brings us back to habituation. If you repeat any exercise over and over, it quickly becomes a habit. How often do you think about the task of tying your shoelaces? How often do you *consciously* brush your teeth? You don't; you just do it! You stand at the sink and think about your 8 o'clock appointment or the call you have to make or which jacket you're going to wear to work. You *don't* think, *brush along the gumline; that's where the plaque forms.*

Thoughts can become habitual, too. If you repeat a thought over and over, the neurons in your brain become so accustomed to focusing and firing in specific ways that they require little coaxing. What happens, for example, is (1) you hear his name; (2) in a nanosecond, you flash back to the day he packed his suitcase; and (3) bang, you're ready to get out the gun.

The Double Whammy

A coworker in your office just got the promotion you've been petitioning to get for a year. The awful part is, she didn't even know to throw her hat in the ring until you told her over lunch one day that the boss was leaving. She thanked you for the tip, went off, and did a better lobbying job than you did. Now *she's* your boss, and you're ready to strangle her. But you can't, of course. You need the job you've got.

What do you do instead? You overeat to distraction, you whine to your friends, and you snap at your kids. You fight with your pillow all night. I call this the double whammy because now you've not only lost the position you dearly coveted, you've also become someone you hate. So who's got the problem? Not your new boss (she's probably sleeping like a baby).

The Quagmire of Negative Thoughts

One of the problems with holding a grudge is how quickly it can take you into negativism and keep you there. Remember the two women who were having lunch at Canyon Ranch? Coincidentally, the younger one, Lois, came to see me the day after I inadvertently overheard their conversation. (It's sometimes hard not to because the tables along the banquette are fairly close together, and that day, mine was directly adjacent to theirs.)

Lois needed some advice. "I've had it up to here with my mother, Dr. Baker," the 27-year-old woman told me, unaware I'd already been acquainted with her situation.

"All she talks about is how my father left her, how she can't forgive him, how he ruined her life. And not only that, but she's trying to take *me* down with her. She's trying to get me to hate him, too!" Her eyes filled with tears. "He's my *father*—or was. He's dead now. So why would I hate him? I mean, what's the point?"

As Lois explained it, her parents were dating when her mother, Harriett, became pregnant, and her father did the honorable thing and married her. Unfortunately, as time would quickly tell, they were a poor match. He was a very easygoing, outgoing man, and Harriett was a classic narcissist. When Lois was 7, her father asked her mother for a divorce so that he could marry a woman with whom he had apparently been involved for years.

That's when her mother started scheming revenge, fueled by regular rehashing of how she'd been wronged. And it was still going strong. All those years. For what?

Thoughts of Revenge Narrow Your Focus

Target acquisition fixation is a state of mind that occurs when the brain focuses on one single thing to the exclusion of everything else. This concept worked for our ancestors because it allowed the hunters to go after their prey undistracted by anything that might try to sideline them. It doesn't always work so well in contemporary times, however.

In the aviation world, target acquisition fixation sometimes affects fighter pilots who are so preoccupied by their target that they lose the sense of who's flying on their right wing, who's flying on their left wing, and who's directly underneath them. This happened to a World War II ace who was flying with my late father-in-law. He was so fixated on blowing up a German plane he had in his sights that he didn't realize that he was only yards above the earth and drove his propeller right into the ground. As a result, he wrecked his plane and was taken as a prisoner of war.

People set on taking revenge get such tunnel vision in trying to destroy their targets that it ruins their peripheral vision. Consequently, they lose sight of anything else going on around them—including the wonderful things life has to offer.

The Victimizing VERB

VERB is an acronym I use to define four situations: victimization, entitlement, rescue, and blame. Any of these, individually or in combination, can cripple your personal power, although at first glance, they may appear to do just the opposite.

- **Victimization.** Let me start by saying I've never met a happy victim. Look, we're all going to have heartache in our lives. Some of us will even have tragedy. The question is, how do you deal with it? Do you wallow in it? Or do you transcend it by channeling it into something that brings meaning to your life or, even better, into the lives of others as well?

Candy Lightner started MADD (Mothers against Drunk Drivers) after a man who was driving drunk killed her daughter. Megan Kanka was kidnapped, sexually assaulted, and murdered by an ex-felon who lived three houses away from her family. Afterward, her mother—and father—worked tirelessly to pass a law that requires informing residents of a neighborhood when a sexual predator moves in. Megan's Law is now active in all 50 states, and her parents continue to crusade for the protection of all children.

They and countless others easily could have chosen to wear the mantle of victimhood. Instead they went on to bring meaning to the legacy of their children and to their own lives by doing something positive.

Happy women understand the importance of having personal power, which means their lives belong to them.

• **Entitlement.** This attitude says, "The world owes me something." We've all seen our share of this. It's often hard to miss in children who've been raised in affluent homes. I'm not saying money is to blame. I've seen highly entitled individuals from middle-class families, too, people who for some reason believe the world owes them a living. Of course, none of us is the center of the universe, and thinking so generally means sitting around being miserable when what we hoped for doesn't come our way. The long and short of it is that entitlement is a stunting, passive approach to life.

Happy women know that taking personal responsibility for what they have and haven't done leads to a powerful and fulfilling way of life.

- **Rescue.** Normally, rescue means saving somebody or something from a dangerous or harmful situation, but when associated with VERBs, it again puts responsibility onto the shoulders of someone else.

One of the women we interviewed for this book had what she called her dream job, producing television shows for a national network. Her job took her to exciting and exotic locations around the world, but after a while, she wanted more. She wanted to be married, have her 2.5 children, and have an existence outside of her career. When she finally met Mr. Right, she decided not to let life pass her by. She left her job to stay closer to home, got married, and had a family. She didn't wait to be rescued; she went out and took life by the horns.

This goes for your career as well. Hate your job? Just know that no one is going to come for you and set you up as president of NBC. You have to do it for yourself.

Happy women know you can't control your destiny,
but you *can* participate in it.

- **Blame.** This is disempowering in that it unloads a sense of responsibility on someone else. That someone else may not give a damn about your welfare, or maybe they couldn't help you *even if they wanted to* because it's not within their power to do so. Blaming someone or something else also means you can't learn from your mistakes. I often use the phrase, "If you paid the tuition, get the lesson."

I never said mistakes aren't painful or costly. But if you talked to Lauren (whom you'll meet in Chapter 6) and asked her what if any mistake she made as she went about selecting a partner, she'd tell you that in choosing her husband, she clearly made a bad choice but that today she is much wiser for it. I have no doubt that knowledge will serve her well in the future.

···

What does VERB have to do with revenge?

It's similar to something called the dead-weight principle. If you're dragging along a 100-pound sandbag called revenge, you aren't taking responsibility for your life. You are a *victim* of your own misery, you feel *entitled* to something better, you are waiting for someone else to *rescue* you, and you can't wait to lay *blame* on the person who put you in that position in the first place.

If you indulge in any of these concepts, just know that you'll expend a lot of energy—and get not an ounce of gain. There is another way. You can employ the following tools, which are certain to make your life better.

It's up to you.

Three Little Words

There is no shortage of reasons that women seek revenge. You could fill a vast library with tabloid stories, novels, movies, and plays driven by revenge. So isn't it amazing that one of the tools for this self-defeating trap can be written on a postage stamp? It can—because it consists of a mere three little words.

Let it go!

I have on my desk a smooth stone a little larger than a golf ball. When someone tells me how someone else "done her wrong," we talk for a while, and then I hand her the stone. I tell her to place it in her dominant hand and squeeze it. "Crush it into talcum powder," I say. Of course, no mere mortal has the hand strength to do so, but she tries; when nothing happens, I tell her to try harder, and again nothing happens. So I say to try even harder. In a few minutes, the muscles of her hand begin to constrict, cutting off the blood supply so her knuckles turn white. At that point, it begins to get uncomfortable, so I tell her to turn her hand downward, open her fingers, and *let the stone go.*

When the stone lands on the floor, I ask, "How do you feel?" My client generally shakes her hand up and down and tells me she feels better. "Aha!" I say. "What you're feeling is relief!"

"I do feel that," she invariably answers.

"Of course you do," I tell her, "because you have let go of something you cannot make the way you want it to be."

That's how forgiveness feels.

You want to be happy again?

Let go of the stone.

Move on.

Get a life.

But first, *forgive.*

First, Forgive

To forgive may be divine, as Alexander Pope would have us believe, but it's hardly easy.

Frederic Luskin, PhD, who directed the Forgiveness Project at Stanford University, says that for your own mental and physical health, forgiving is essential. In his book *Forgive for Good,* Dr. Luskin makes the distinction between forgiveness and condoning actions, forgetting them, or reconciling with the offender. None of the last three, he says, may be possible. But obsessing over grievances against others makes it impossible to get on with your life. It is only through forgiveness that we can let go, stop playing the role of victim, and move on.

Unresolved anger is a very expensive emotion and one that anyone I've ever met can ill afford. I addressed this very issue with a woman not too long ago. Mickey is a buyer at a large department store chain in California, married to a dentist. She was dropping his suit off at the cleaners and discovered a woman's business card in his jacket pocket. It wouldn't have been memorable perhaps, except that it had the woman's cell phone number written on it—and smelled of perfume. The *coup de grâce* was that the card belonged to her best friend.

I have heard multiple stories like this; we all have: the husband and the wife's best friend, or the wife and the husband's best friend. It's tough to forgive because it's a double blow, like being hit in the face with a baseball bat—twice. You begin to understand that the people you imagined you knew don't exist. This woman imagined her husband to be faithful. She imagined her friend to be supportive, with her best interest in mind. But the truth is, if she has been a good friend and a loyal spouse, she deserves better in her life than what she has gotten from those people. In a manner of speaking, they've done her a favor, even if it takes a while—and it may take years—for her to believe that. Now she has the chance, albeit one she hardly welcomes, to look for somebody new who is honest and a true friend or partner.

When she came to see me, distraught about the whole situation, I sympathized. It was, after all, a 12-year marriage, and she really loved the guy. It's never easy to separate the rational from the emotional, particularly in the early days when the sting is still there, but I tried my best. I asked her to close her eyes and imagine a scenario.

"Mickey," I said, "do you have a savings account?"

"Yes."

"Good. I'd like you to go down to the bank and withdraw all your money in $1 bills. Take whatever amount of money you have out of the account, get in your car, drive down the main street of your town, and start tossing the money out the window by the fistful."

"What does that have to do with anything?"

"Well, think about it. Would you ever really do that?"

"No!"

"Of course not. Now how much more valuable is your life's energy?" I asked. "Why would you choose to throw something so valuable away on someone who doesn't deserve it?"

Mickey got the point, and she agreed with it in principle, but remembering it when she needed some help wasn't going to be that easy. In such heartbreaking cases, it never is.

How do you forgive a cheating spouse, a trusted friend who betrayed you, or a boss who is killing your chances for promotion? Do you refuse to forgive an unreasonable act because you believe to do so is to sanction the injury? If that's the case, you need to understand that forgiving is not at all about sanctioning. It is about giving *yourself* a gift.

Happy women know that forgiving doesn't let the offender
off the hook; it lets *you* off the hook.

Why It's Easier to Forgive Than to Forget

You'll notice that all this time I've been invoking forgiveness, not once did I pair it with the word *forget*. That's because I don't expect you to forget something that made you desperately unhappy. We can't forget a wrong any more than we can make the sun rise when we want it to. Even if we're halfway around the globe and 50 years hence, we can't forget.

Nature deemed it so. She wrapped up all our memories and parked the unpleasant ones—even those we deeply wish to forget—in a walnut-size part of the lower midbrain called the *amygdala*.

This is where we store our emotional memories. Eons ago, the amygdala formed as a protective mechanism to ensure survival of the species, and it did its job well.

Here's how it works: Let's say a group of your ancestors are taking a leisurely stroll across the African Savannah 70,000 years ago. As they travel, they detect slight movement in the grass 20 paces in front of them. Two weeks before, when the grass moved like that, it was due to a poisonous snake, its gaze trained in their direction. Everyone turned and ran, except one member of their party, who had been in the front of the group. She emerged from the grass with a serious snakebite on her ankle. This time, the amygdala remembers, so when the travelers see the grass move, they react 2 seconds faster, and because they do, they all make it home safely.

The amygdala is about sensing danger. It reminds us in a split second about things that might hurt or kill us. It has put fear into us, and sometimes we still need that fear. When a pot has been sitting over a gas flame for an hour, we know not to touch it until it cools.

But leading our lives in fear generally doesn't serve us well.

Most of the time, we could do nicely without it, thank you. But alas, we're hardwired to route such things through the amygdala, and we need to understand that it's going to be with us no matter what. We need to consciously manage it for a more meaningful life.

In *Happiness: The Science behind Your Smile,* Daniel Nettle, PhD, a lecturer in psychology at the University of Newcastle in England, calls this a fear program. He points out that while it triggers embarrassing reactions—such as "hiding under our seats whilst watching the film *Jurassic Park*"—it has been advantageous over evolutionary time. He writes:

> People today are more afraid of Mad Cow epidemics and spiders than they are of electrical sockets and automobiles, which statistically is totally senseless. We are much more likely to be killed in an accident while driving during the course of one month than we are from eating infected beef in our entire lifetime.

The impact of the amygdala is ubiquitous. I was playing golf one beautiful Arizona afternoon with a buddy from the Vietnam War. It was the Fourth of July. We were on the 18th green next to the clubhouse, and my buddy was putting out. A kid near the clubhouse lit a string of firecrackers and they went off, sounding exactly like machine gun fire. The minute my buddy heard the sound, he hit the deck. That's the amygdala at work. It was 35 years after the war, and he was still having uninvited flashbacks.

A flashback is a reactive memory that occurs when the amygdala sends out a red alert, *even when the alert is cued by something that is not dangerous*. We respond with lightning speed, and that's what (potentially) saves us—we don't take time to reason. We just react as if it were the real thing, and that's the amygdala at its very best. It doesn't let us forget. Unfortunately, it doesn't let Lois's mother, Harriet, forget either. But she can get better. She can begin with some of the tools below, but she also has to stop hating.

In the end, hate is fear. We hate the people who hurt us, but that's only because we're so fearful they will hurt us again. To hate someone is to give them power. But remember, we gave that power away—and we can take it back.

To hate is easy, and so is to love, but love and hate cannot live in the same heart. You must make the choice for yourself. It's simple; it's only a choice.

Barring anything else, I suggest that a woman take what I call the tombstone test. Quite simply, it asks you to think about what you would want on your tombstone. Do you want it to read, "She was a vindictive, hateful woman" or "She was a loving, caring human being"? How do you want to be remembered?

Plan now, for later.

Forgiving Yourself

Sometimes the most difficult type of forgiveness is the one that's required when you're angry with yourself. Sometimes we all do stupid things in retaliation. How many times have you sabotaged yourself and wondered why? It may have to do with wanting revenge against yourself for making a grievous error—one that you don't even remember. You feel remorse and beat yourself up. *How could I be so stupid?* you ask yourself, with no answer in mind. Then you go off to the nearest bakery and indulge in a dozen chocolate chip cookies. For a few minutes, you feel better because you've taken your mind off your error and put it onto the cookies. After the last bite, though, you feel worse because you've not only made a mistake that you don't even remember, but you've lost control and eaten far too many of things you resolved only yesterday to do without. Go figure.

I once knew a woman who, like me, came of age in the 1960s. Bunny became a feminist in the 1970s, and by the 1980s, when I met her, she had earnestly invested in the idea that she could do or be *anything* she wanted. "I *can* have it all," was her mantra. Bunny not only held aloft the banner of feminism, she led the whole parade. With a well-worn copy of *The Feminine Mystique* under her arm, she joined a consciousness-raising group of women in search of more meaningful lives.

Although they never burned their bras, these women cheered each other on. They believed and fought for equal rights and equal pay. They didn't shave their legs and underarms, scoffed at men who opened doors for them, and marched in endless parades, telling themselves the point was to ensure equality for their daughters. Much of this was in fact tremendously worthwhile—but not all of it.

One evening, just after dinner, Bunny took off her apron and announced to her family that life was calling her, and she wanted to taste it. She *deserved* her chance. She needed to be free.

She never considered what effect following her dream would have on the husband and 7-year-old daughter she left behind. She just packed up and left.

Five years and many failed dreams later, she realized what she had done. In my office, through a torrent of tears, she wailed, "I sabotaged myself, Dr. Baker. *And for what?* There was nothing out there for me. My daughter had all those years without a mother. I ruined my husband's life. I ruined my own, too. How do I go on?"

Instead of finding the wholly fulfilling life she'd imagined, she'd found remorse. We talked about it, and I explained that sometimes the hardest thing in the world to do is be kind to ourselves. Forgiving oneself can take an earth-shattering, mind-altering, gut-wrenching awakening, but if you're ever to have a meaningful life, it must be done.

"You did an impulsive thing," I said. "You're a flawed, flesh-and-blood human being who was caught up in an emotional situation. Now you understand the power of an impulse. It's a strong, primitive response. You were actually protecting yourself, doing what you thought you needed to do. And you made a mistake."

I suggested that rather than berate herself, it would be far more constructive to ask, *How can I learn from this? What lessons can I take away?*

Here are the lessons I would wish for Bunny.

- Every decision we make has a consequence.
- Every decision we make is an experiment. We often think we know what the outcome will be, but sometimes we are a little off, and sometimes we are a lot off. The ultimate goal, no matter what the outcome, is to learn and grow wise. You can't develop wisdom in a negative environment. Wisdom requires nurturance.
- If we learn from as many of life's experiences as possible, we will make better decisions over time. The quality of life is determined by the sum total of the consequences of all the decisions we've ever made.

• When people say life is a journey, not a destination, learning life's answers is what the journey is all about.

Every one of us makes mistakes, and they are often self-sabotaging ones. Forgiveness comes when you can say, "I made a big mistake. I learned a lot. I'm smarter and wiser. I won't do that one again. Let's move on."

Happy women understand the three steps
to self-forgiveness:

• Acknowledge the lesson you learned.
• Recognize that you're now in a different place.
• Know that you may make a new mistake tomorrow.

More Tools to Dig Yourself Out of That Rut

Clearly, forgiveness is the primary gift you can give yourself, as it assures the benefit of freeing yourself from obsession with revenge. But there are other tactics that can work almost as well. Here are three that I have found to be very successful.

Get Him to Zero

If Harriet instead of her daughter, Lois, had come to me, I would have said this to her: "You know that ex-husband who has made you so miserable that you're still dreaming of ways to settle the score? Okay, let's say that despite all efforts, you absolutely, positively refuse to forgive him. In that case, you do have another choice. With a little bit of self-determination, you can make this person a nonentity. After all, you're still furious and hateful and thinking he's the worst thing that ever happened to you. Isn't it counterproductive to also make him central to your life? Move him on out!"

Here's how: Think of a scale from minus 20 to plus 20. It's your personal scale. At the negative end is the worst form of dislike—hate, if you will. At the positive end, at plus 20, is love.

If you hate, you're bathing yourself in negative emotion. You're expending energy on someone you already know is not worth it. Energy is finite. If you show up too often at the teller's window, the bank account soon runs dry. Negative emotion is also bad for your health, bad for your face (stress causes wrinkles), and bad for your relationships with the people you care about (who wants to spend time with someone who goes on and on about something that happened in the past?).

At the other end is love, the ultimate in positive emotion. It's where you flourish and enjoy a meaningful life, where you receive energy from time spent on yourself and with friends you enjoy.

So where on the scale does Mr. Wrong belong? Not on the negative end, because he's not worth expending energy on, not a single atom's worth. Not on the plus side, because he clearly hasn't earned a spot there. So take him to zero—and keep him there. In your conscious mind, over which you do have control, make him nothing, *nada*, zip. Every time your brain conjures up his name, just deposit him at the center of the scale and leave him there and go on with your day. He can't bother you anymore.

Zero is nothing. Don't forget it.

Here's another take on the same theme. This is the message I would hammer home to Harriet, given the chance.

"Do you love your daughter?"

"Yes, of course."

"How much do you love her?"

"With all my heart and soul."

"So, you once had a life with someone who behaved badly. He also contributed to the fact that your beloved daughter now walks the face of this

Earth. The truth is, she wouldn't be here if it weren't for him coming into your life. So what do a big minus and a big plus of the same magnitude add up to? Why, zero, of course."

Go Out and Engage Life

Engaging life is a constructive diversion. For something that has a far better payback, try doing something for someone else in need. At the very least, you'll help some soul in this universe have a little more comfort in life. And wouldn't you rather build your life around something constructive as opposed to something destructive? I really believe that the vast majority of humans are by nature constructive beings. We want to build families, neighborhoods, and relationships.

The reason we entertain destructive thoughts is fear. If terrorists had no fear of Western thought and culture, they would never attack. Go out and get involved. Build something—something meaningful to you and someone else. Have a life that's so full that you don't have time to think about the person who hurt you and what was done to you.

Have a Starbucks Date with Yourself

Or go somewhere else where you can sit quietly and have a cup of coffee. Oh, have biscotti, too. Why not? You need to have a heart-to-heart chat with yourself, and here are the questions you must ask.

- What kind of person do I want to be? Am I going to allow this other person's behavior, indiscretion, or judgment to turn me into something less than I was before?
- I'm only here for a certain amount of time. Do I want to spend the remaining years of my life ruminating about revenge?
- Am I really a nasty, mean-spirited person? If I'm not, but I'm rehearsing mean-spirited nastiness, I'm at odds with my authentic

self. And that means I take myself to war. Is this person worth taking myself to war?

* If there are children in my life, do I want them to learn how to handle hurt and adversity with dignity and grace? To understand that if they ever need to, they can rise above a bad situation? Am I setting a good example for them?

Suzanne Mikols could have answered those questions in a heartbeat. She had not even heard of positive psychology, but she could be a poster child for the movement. She instinctively practiced some of the most important principles.

When she awoke after her accident and found herself in the intensive care unit of a local hospital, her thoughts were fuzzy, her balance was totally off, her limbs were sore, and her head was killing her. Several days later, when she could think a little more clearly, she knew she had some decisions to make about her future. Would she consider herself a victim and spend even 5 minutes of precious energy on the man who changed her life? Not a chance. She was a survivor. The word *victim* was not in her lexicon. So what did she do?

The first business at hand was to focus on building her strengths—both physical and emotional—and capitalizing on them to accelerate her return to a normal life. A full return may never happen—her damaged brain has seen to that—but she possesses an abundance of the key ingredients for bouncing back, and these will carry her far.

She has optimism, which led her to set goals beyond her reach. Working just that little bit harder than was required got her moving all the sooner. That same optimism has been essential in warding off depression, which, after a debilitating accident and in the face of such a long recovery, might be expected to come knocking on the door of even the most cheerful of women.

She chose not to focus on the past or the future, knowing it didn't matter. Her classic answer to questions about her long-term plans was always the same: "I have no idea what the future will bring, so why even go there?"

She took little Kaizen steps each day, always seeking new possibilities, and was thrilled by the small successes of her first shower, her first stroll outside, her first car ride, and then driving again. She appreciated the friendship of those around her and allowed them to assist her when she needed help.

The most important thing, however, was that never once during the trauma of her long recovery did she think of herself as a victim. As a result, she never visited the concept of revenge. Suzanne Mikols didn't just survive; she thrived.

CHAPTER SIX

I'm Nothing without Him

*No one can make you feel inferior
without your consent.*

Eleanor Roosevelt

Everyone hits a rough patch now and then, but some patches are rougher than others. Ever feel so sure of the ground under your feet that you never even bother to look down, until one day it falls out from under you? This is what it feels like when you place *who you are* in the hands of another person, and that person decides he doesn't want the responsibility—or worse, he decides he no longer wants you.

Whether a breakup is a slow deterioration or strikes like a bolt of lightning, it's a real crisis. And when your identity is completely enmeshed with that other person, it's even worse. The very moment you realize it's really over, there is no *you* left to protect yourself. Your normal expectations, your assumptions, and your self-perception are squashed. It's a phenomenon that W. Keith Campbell, PhD, associate professor of psychology at the University of Georgia, calls ego shock.

You are now left to pick up the pieces and rebuild your life without him. But first you have to find *yourself* again.

Women and Relationships

There are many types of relationships in this world. Ironically, the ones that are most difficult to rebound from are those that were never true partnerships to begin with. The reason so many women remain in such unbalanced relationships—she gives, he takes—is simply that they are afraid of what life would be like without a man.

Some say women are socialized to believe that they'll live lesser lives on their own. Others would argue that it's the urge to partner up—yet another gift from our ancestors—or that it's good old fear raising its ugly head once again. I'm not a betting man, but I'd have to put my money on three and two to win and place. And if there's anything left over, I'd lay it on number one to show.

You've seen again and again that fear is essential for our survival. Our ancestors who kept looking over their shoulders in an attempt to anticipate a predator's next attack—that is, the ones who played it safest—were the ones most likely to stay around long enough to pass on their genes. Because *they* were fearful, we are fearful as well.

Thanks, Grandma, but no thanks.

While fear helped ensure our ancestors' survival, it doesn't always serve us in the modern world, particularly for women when it comes to venturing out on their own. Fear of an unknown future can keep anyone frozen in place, and that's what happens to many women in untenable relationships. They're scared to depart from the familiar, because what if the unknown is worse than what they have in hand?

I call this the prison of fear.

No one needs to remain locked up, though. All it takes to free yourself is an understanding of how our brains respond to fear.

Fear is all about the future. We fear only those things that have not happened because we don't know what impact they will have on our lives. Wouldn't it be great if we could predict the future? We'd feel in control and secure. Of course, that's impossible; no one can predict anything 100 percent accurately, so given the choice, we stick with what we know. The more familiar something is, the more we feel we can predict what will happen next, and consequently, the less fear we will have. Alas, it's a vicious cycle.

After 35 years in this business, I can say with some authority that there isn't a relationship in the world a woman can't walk away from if she has courage and a good pair of shoes. Despite the tremendous strides women have made in the past century, however, it turns out that fear often prevails, and women simply don't take that first step. In this primarily coupled world, they are afraid they can't make it on their own.

It's So Nice to Have a Man around the Cave

Actually, in the Stone Age, it was more than just *nice*. It was essential. Historically, men were the stronger and more dominant sex. If you didn't have a man around the cave to protect, feed, and care for you, you probably weren't going to make it. Equally important, if you wanted to hand down your genetic material, you needed a man for procreation.

While Sally Stoneage probably didn't sit around the fire ruminating about her biological clock, she did want to have as many children as she could. Children were an essential and instinctive part of our ancestors' lives because beyond bringing joy, children had an important role to play. They were younger and stronger and could help and protect their parents as the parents began to age. Beginning in the 17th and 18th centuries, more than 90 percent of all jobs were agrarian. People had huge families in part so they would have enough help with all the work.

Like us contemporary mortals, Sally found sex—along with eating—among the most pleasurable events of the day. Sex made her happy and babies made her happy, which meant that men were essential because back then, it still took two to tango. Today, a good doctor, a good freezer, and several petri dishes mean there's hardly a need for a man anymore. (Give us another generation, and there will probably be no need for either a male or a female to produce a baby.)

Even as recently as the 1800s, men were still an indispensable part of women's lives. That's part of the rationale behind the polygamy movement in this country. It is thought that one reason polygamy got started in the Church of Latter Day Saints sect was that during the trek from Missouri across the plains to Utah, so many of the men were killed or injured that when the travelers arrived at their new homeland, the men were greatly outnumbered. The Mormon Church may have looked at the four-women-to-one-man situation and decided a good solution was to let a man take multiple wives.

The justification was that this practice was fairly common in biblical times. As for the women, many believed—and still do—that it was better to have a time-share man than no man at all.

A Tale of Three Women

Phyllis, Lauren, and Kate are women in their fifties, forties, and thirties, respectively. Phyllis and Lauren were guests at the ranch. I met Kate through a mutual friend, and later, she shared her story.

All of these women were on the receiving end of painful breakups. All three were devastated and could have easily fallen into the trap of believing they were nothing without "him."

Phyllis

Life was just perfect for Phyllis—she made sure of it. She was living in the mansion of her dreams in Morristown, New Jersey. She had a membership in the "right" country club and a first-tier box at the symphony. She wore Cartier watches and artfully draped Hermes scarves over her Prada dresses. Married to Harvey, one of New Jersey's most prominent surgeons, she embraced the status conferred on her. He was "Dr. X" and she was "Mrs. Doctor." Yes, life was perfect—until one day, he packed up and left.

Six months after Alan's untimely exit, Phyllis showed up at the ranch. I had met her a while before, when she and Harvey were guests at the Life Enhancement Center. I remembered him as a serious but likeable man. I didn't remember her quite as well.

She strode into my office, sat down, and started talking to me as if we had seen each other very recently. I had barely said hello when she launched into her story. "You're not going to believe this, Dr. Baker," she said, then proceeded to describe how she and her 18-year-old daughter had returned from a Paris shopping trip one Sunday to find that Alan had moved out, lock, stock, and bank account. "How could he *do* this to me?" she wailed. "He killed me! I have *no* life anymore. I'm nothing!"

I couldn't help but think of Shakespeare's line, "Hell hath no fury like a woman scorned." Old "Wills" must have known someone just like Phyllis.

"You're nothing?" I asked, handing her a box of tissues. "I'm sitting across from you, and I'm seeing a lot. I'm seeing a mother, a daughter, a sister, and if I remember correctly, a damn good golfer."

She looked up at me in surprise. "Don't you see? That's part of it. The SOB resigned from the club. I can't go there any more. I have to play on the public course. It's humiliating."

I'd heard worse, but I listened as she continued, a bit softer now. "I want my old life back! I want to be happy again."

As she went on, the picture became crystal clear. Phyllis equated being happy with being Mrs. Doctor, with all the trappings that position afforded her.

Sometimes it's what a person *doesn't* say that speaks volumes. I have to insert here that never in the hour we spent together did she mention missing or wanting him. Alan was clearly not her priority, which may be (I'm guessing here) a very large part of the reason that he left her.

I listened as she complained about being the lone single in a world of married friends. About feeling ugly and old. No one would ask her out. None of her friends were fixing her up, so she was certain she'd never find anyone else ever again.

"Phyllis," I said, "how appealing do you think you are as a companion right now? How enjoyable is it to be in your company?"

She muttered, "I don't know. Probably not very."

"That's right. And that's because you're beating up on yourself. You're at war with yourself," I told her. "If this is the face you show the world, you'll scare off any decent prospect, or worse, you'll attract the sharks."

Phyllis's story reinforced what we already know. Because negative emotions in all of us are so much stronger than positive ones, when a lover rejects us, we think no one else in the world will ever find us attractive. (And yet, if we win a round of golf, we don't then conclude we'll win every match we play.)

I tried to explain this to Phyllis and tell her the importance of moving on, but she didn't (and maybe couldn't at that point) hear me. She was completely and utterly focused on a single word: *alone.*

Divorce is an unfortunately common occurrence, but there are people who take that opportunity to go forward toward more meaningful lives. They look for new friends, move to a new town, find good work to do. Others turn to drugs or alcohol or just crawl into their own shells—another misfortune because that just compounds the misery. Women like Phyllis who abandon themselves are very unhappy people. They put themselves down. They neglect themselves. And yes, they *are* alone—if only in their heads.

Let's make a distinction here. Happy women enjoy solitude, which is enjoying life's pleasures in a most simplistic context. When happy women are alone, they don't feel isolated from their families, their friends, or their coworkers because they know those people are there if they want them. Happy women know they can walk back into a world of people in a minute, an hour, or a day—whenever they want to. Lonely women feel isolated, cut off, and apart from other human beings. They never know if they will have someone to return to, and as a result, they become hopeless. Again, you can't be happy and hopeless at the same time.

> Happy women are never alone because they
> don't abandon themselves.

Connection is all-important to a full and meaningful life, and we'll address this in depth in Chapter 9.

Women are so other-directed that they often overlook the relationship they have with themselves. If I said to you, "Tell me about the relationship you have with your husband, with your boyfriend, with your parents, with your children," you'd be off and running. If I asked you to tell me about the relationship you have with yourself, could you do it? You could, but you'd probably have to think about it. The reason you'd have to think about it is that you *don't* think about it on a regular basis.

Self-relating is perhaps one of the most important concepts of psychology because that's where this whole identity notion starts. Phyllis couldn't create a life for herself because she didn't know who *she* was. And that's because there *was* no Phyllis, only Mrs. Doctor. She had developed nothing else in the 20 years of her married life, so it should have come as no surprise that when Alan left her, Phyllis's identity followed him out the door.

Writing about self-image in the journal *Social Cognition*, Duke University psychologist Patricia Linville, PhD, cautions against putting all your eggs in one basket. She explains that the more multidimensional a person is, the happier she is, whether life has dealt her an unexpected blow or a boost. It stands to reason. If Jane Doe is a famous chef but *only* a chef, and she loses her job, that's it. But if she's a chef and a writer and a cooking teacher and a Girl Scout leader, her identity and self-image are only partially affected by her job loss. I call this a diversified psychological portfolio.

Think about it: Your investment counselor would never tell you to invest all your money in a single stock—nor should you invest all your emotional and creative energy in one person or thing. Instead, diversify, diversify, diversify!

I wish I could tell you that I succeeded in helping Phyllis, but sometimes I empty my bag of tricks and find that nothing works. From what I could see, she left the ranch as unhappy as she was when she arrived, but then some people just aren't ready to give up their misery, so perhaps in the end, she was precisely where she wanted to be.

Lauren

To the outside world, Lauren had it all: good looks, a great job as development director of a symphony orchestra, a wonderful marriage to a stock analyst. In fact, though, for the past 11 years, Lauren had kept a terrible secret.

The first time I met Lauren, she had come to the ranch for a 3-day retreat with her twin sister. She was a wiry woman with long blonde hair and was fast-talking, fidgety, and uncomfortable. I wasn't at all sure she wanted to be in my office.

This happens sometimes. When people check into the ranch, one of the cadres of program advisors conducts an interview to see if there's some way to enhance their stay. The advisor listens for certain things to see which programs might best suit that particular guest. If they hear something that they believe lines up with what I do, they ask if the guest would be interested in seeing me.

In a handful of cases, people come into my office and say, "I don't know why I'm here. I feel pretty good." And I tell them that is the great part about their coming. I suggest we explore what they did to feel good and then focus on how they can keep that going for as long as possible. After some preliminary discussion, that's exactly what Lauren and I talked about—when life had been best for her.

For a split second, I noticed just the slightest hint of tightness in her lips, then a hesitation. Her reply was vague, as if there were something she wanted to say but couldn't. From my experience, these very subtle signs tell me something is probably amiss. So I asked her the very simple question that often elicits the information I'm seeking: "Do you feel safe at home?"

Six words. And, as I thought they might, the floodgates opened.

She talked and talked, and I listened yet again to words that were all too familiar. Words that assembled themselves to vividly portray a classic and accelerating case of spousal abuse, both mental and physical.

Lauren said she tried everything to make her husband, David, happy. Thinking *he* would change if *she* did, she bleached her hair to look sexier, stopped seeing friends he didn't like, and saw her twin sister only when he was at work. I explained to her that she could have walked on water, and it wouldn't have mattered. He's not going to be happy with her because *she's* not the one he hates. He hates himself. It doesn't matter what she does or whom she turns herself into. It won't work.

In keeping with the principles of positive psychology, when I meet a woman who has fallen into this trap, I don't ask her to dwell on the painful parts. Instead I asked Lauren, as I had also asked Phyllis, a few questions designed to help her move forward by raising her awareness.

- How would you characterize the price you're paying for doing what you're doing?
- Is what you're doing working?
- Is this how you want to live your life?

To drive home the point, I told Lauren to visualize the two of us going scuba diving. "You have a small tank of oxygen, and I have a large one. We dive deep. At around 200 feet, you run out of air. So you look at me and indicate that you may need some of my air, and I say, 'If you want some of my air, you have to do everything I want you to do.' " That's the position you're in with David. Do you really want to treat love as if it's air?"

It was 2 years before I saw Lauren again. She was visiting the ranch and dropped by my office to say hello. Her once-blonde hair was now dark brown. She was tanned, had gained some weight, and looked wonderful. She was a calmer, more serene Lauren than I remembered—a Lauren clearly at peace.

I was pleased to see this transformation and told her so. "How's life?" I asked.

She informed me she had left David and moved into her own apartment. "Good for you," I said, because when I saw her last, she told me she didn't think she'd ever have the guts to leave him. I asked how she had summoned the courage.

"Actually, Dr. Baker, I think I began to see things clearly after I spoke to you. It was here in this office that I heard myself admit for the first time how bad things really were. And I suppose I began to think about what I might need to do. God, I was scared. But then, a few weeks after I got home, I had sort of an epiphany."

"An epiphany?"

"Yes. I was sitting in my kitchen having a cup of coffee with my sister and laughing about old times, when I heard David's key slide into the front door lock. That sound set me into action like a starter's pistol. I jumped up from the table to make sure the kitchen was perfect. No crumbs on the counter, dishtowels folded just so. As he came into the house, I quickly took his coat and brought him the mail. My sister described to me later that the abrupt change in me was astonishing. She said it was as if I had suddenly morphed into a Stepford wife on speed."

"Then what?"

"She left a few minutes later, and David and I lapsed directly into one of the scenarios that had become all too common. I fixed him a martini ("not enough gin—what the hell's the matter with you?") Made him dinner ("for God's sake, do you have to burn every goddamn thing you make?"). I had just had my hair cut really short that afternoon, and I thought I looked really nice, so I asked him if he liked it. With that, he grabbed me by the arm, pulled me to the dining room mirror, and practically shoved my face into it. 'Whoever did this should be shot,' he said, then stormed out of the house, headed for a bar where 'someone knows how to make a *real* martini.'

"I never knew what set him off. But after he left, I stood in front of that mirror for I don't know how long, staring at a twisted face surrounding the saddest eyes I had ever seen. And that's when I finally admitted to myself what was really happening. What I saw looking back was not me, Dr. Baker. It was my future."

Why Stay?

How does it happen that a woman who seemingly has everything going for her falls into the dreadful den of an abuser and worse, remains there?

Sometimes it happens because the truth is often too awful to acknowl-edge: You've made a terrible mistake; he led you to believe he was some-thing he wasn't, and you fell for it. Sometimes it's because you don't want to worry your loved ones, or you don't want to upset the family, or it's easier to cover things up than to face the truth.

Very often a woman stays because she believes that she is the cause, that she isn't being or doing the right thing and thus deserves the abuse. In a way, that gives her some power over the situation. If she believes she brought the abuse on herself, then she also has the power to make it better with the right words or the perfect meal. But that's an erroneous assump-tion to start with. You're half of every relationship you're in, but only half. You can't control or change the other half no matter how good your inten-tions are, unless, of course, he wants it—and that goes for your children, too.

Most often, I've found, the reason women stay trapped in painful situa-tions is that *the devil they know is preferable to the devil they don't know.* In other words, they stay because it's preferable to what they see as an even more desolate and difficult life without their partners.

We could all give our power away to someone else because we want love and want to be taken care of. But let's not forget: They didn't take it from us. We had to give it to them.

Drawing from a Well of Courage

If a woman is in an abusive situation and doesn't do something to help herself, she's an enabler, and that's sufficient to make anyone miserable. It's as if you're calling the wrath of some maniac upon yourself because you didn't have the courage to say, "That's enough!"

Psychologist Martin Seligman, PhD, would define this type of woman as a pessimist. He says that pessimists trip over three Ps. They take any bad situation *personally*, they see it as *pervasive* in all aspects of life, and they believe it's *permanent*.

> Happy women never see a bad situation as pervasive or permanent—and they don't take it personally.

Every mutually supportive relationship is dynamic, meaning that at one time or another, one party is getting more than the other. A viable relationship can be expected to ebb and flow, but when it's *always* imbalanced, and you *always* feel you're being drained of energy, that's not healthy.

It takes a lot of courage to leave a relationship, and I know many women who can't summon up that courage, but they are not happy women.

For sure, there are going to be situations where leaving requires a leap of faith. There are no guarantees of a happy life on the outside. In fact, no one can guarantee anything. But I can promise you this: If you remove yourself from an abusive situation, if you're willing to try life on your own, *you're not going to get beaten up anymore.*

You can summon courage if you want to, because like fear, it is programmed into your brain. Unlike fear, though, which resides in the primitive reptilian brain, courage resides in the neocortex, the modern brain that is the seat of intellect, spirit, and high emotion. Because courage emanates from the top third of the brain, it already has a leg up on fear. In a game of "can you top this," courage wins every time.

As you saw earlier, there are three parts of the brain that have evolved over time. The oldest is the brainstem, which is formed in the womb and was found in animals more than 100 million years ago. Reptiles have only brainstems and lower brains, which is why the primitive part of the brain is sometimes called the reptilian brain. This is the home of instinct, which drives snakes to strike out when someone comes near. A snake doesn't stop and consider if the women in the colorful beads might be predators because a snake doesn't think. It reacts instinctively. A deer freezes in the forest when it hears an approaching footstep for the same reason.

The second part of the brain to develop was the mammalian brain. This is the area that houses the amygdala, which we spoke of earlier. This small, almond-shaped area in the middle brain acts as a watchdog by warehousing memories of anything that has ever scared us in the past, even the stuff we dearly wish to forget. It's because of the amygdala that you know to beware of fire, violent storms, and big things bearing down on you. You don't have to think about keeping your fingers away from a hot pan. Once burned, twice shy, as the saying goes.

The third part of the brain to evolve—and this is where humans are separated from animals—was the neocortex. The neocortex is the last brain area to develop in the womb and is the site of intellect. Abstract reasoning and memory reside there; so does the spirit. It is the part of the brain that helps us reason and take action in our own best interest. As you read these words, the neurons, synapses, and dendrites in your neocortex are having a field day. Well, then, you may ask, if the neocortex trumps the mammalian brain, and fear resides in the mammalian brain, why am I still so blindsided by fear?

It's because fear comes automatically, readily, and easily. You have to have a level of consciousness and intention to evoke the higher or moral brain to overtake the two lower brains and act in a more rational way. And this I call courage. This is why firefighters rehearse what they're going to do in combative situations. In the face of a blaze, they continue to perform in the manner in which they were trained. This is why during 9/11, confronting an impossible task, they ran into rather than out of the burning building. They went up to get people out.

Even though the amygdala was telling them to "get the hell out of there; there's nothing you can do," they overrode that. They decided they were going to go in and get out as many people as they could—and some of them paid with their lives for the decision. But it was a conscious decision. If they had *reacted* rather than acting consciously, they would not have been inside that building, and people probably wouldn't have blamed them for running out—they were, after all, on the first floor. But they didn't leave. And this is why the neocortex is called the higher-order, moral brain: It overrides the basic instinctive, fear-driven reaction.

This is courage.

As for Lauren, who won the courageous woman of the week award, she told me later that while she wished the situation with David had not been so difficult and destructive, she felt she was a stronger and better person for finally summoning the courage to leave him. "And I have never been so in love with life," she said. "Who would have thought?"

I would.

> Happy women know that courage is taking
> constructive action in spite of fear.

Kate

Kate, a young woman who works in the media, has always been an optimist, but like the rest of us, she's had her share of heartache. We were introduced by a mutual friend, and one day, we got to talking. I told her that I was working on a book about happy women. I explained that I was interviewing a number of women from across the country who overcame adverse situations to emerge happier and better people on the other side.

"Well, here's one you might want to use," she said, and she proceeded to tell me the following story.

She'd been dating "John Doe" for 11 months when he "informally" proposed marriage. "Well, he hadn't exactly *proposed*," she told me, "but we were discussing which area of the city to move to and which baby names went best with his last name. Wouldn't that make you think he had marriage in mind?"

On Valentine's Day weekend, when she was convinced he'd make it official, he took her to a beautiful Vermont resort for a ski vacation. There, while swinging from a ski lift high atop a snow-covered mountain, he made an announcement: Lately he had been hearing this little "voice" in his head, a voice that told him she was not the right one for him. He was terribly sorry, he said. It wasn't easy for him to tell her this, but it was over.

"Talk about being left dangling," Kate said. "I felt like a novice tightrope walker with a sudden attack of vertigo. His timing couldn't have been worse."

She was devastated, and going back home meant a 4½-hour drive with him. Two hundred miles worth of tears and tissues all the way back to New York.

She told me it took a full 2 weeks for her tears to subside, and on the very day they did, her telephone rang. He had made the biggest mistake of his life, he said. Could she ever forgive him? Would she please, please, *please* take him back?

"After minor consideration—okay, the truth is, maybe I thought about it for 10 minutes—I agreed. That evening, he came to my apartment and we had a passionate reunion. But sometime well before midnight, he began shaking his head. He didn't understand it, but there was that *damn* little voice again."

How did Kate respond? She knew the power she needed to live the life she wanted rested nowhere but inside her. Accordingly, she took her cue from Ivana Trump. She didn't get mad; she got rich. She wrote a book about the whole experience, saw it published to terrific reviews, and had the first copy hand delivered to him at his office. A movie script is in the works.

> Happy women know that that happiness is not the art
> of building a trouble-free life but rather the art of
> responding well when trouble strikes.

Responding well has everything to do with a positive attitude, and Kate had that in spades. Studies show that when people use coping strategies successfully, they develop feelings of self-worth and pride. Research also shows that when feelings of self-worth occur, the body releases a number of chemicals, including the neurotransmitter norepinephrine, which produces feelings of happiness.

Unlike Phyllis, Kate looked at what was right and good in her life. And because I always believe you find what you go looking for, I'm not surprised that she found it. Sure, she had a rough time for a while, but on those days, she quietly called on her support system of family and friends to help her through. Did she worry about never attracting another man? Not Kate. She was too busy dating again.

Attitude and Happiness: The Perfect Merger

Kate was an optimist, and as you saw earlier in this chapter, optimists don't see things as all-pervasive or permanent, and she didn't take it personally. (After getting over the initial shock, she decided it was his loss, and she moved on.) Likewise Suzanne Mikols, about whom you read in Chapter 5. Suzanne didn't take it personally when a drug addict fell asleep at the wheel and plowed his car into hers. She never held him personally responsible. She knew that her energy had been compromised and that she had to focus what energy she had on getting better. That's an optimist.

Attitude is hugely important in determining the subjective quality of life because it influences how you interpret the events around you. Consider the theory of Albert Ellis, PhD, a pioneer in the area of cognitive therapy.

Back in the 1960s, Dr. Ellis developed what he referred to as the ABC model. The idea was to use this model to describe events that lead to the feelings we experience.

A is the activating event or the experience you encounter. B is the belief through which you interpret that event (i.e., your attitude), and C represents the consequences of A and B—that is, your feelings associated with the event. Because A—a specific experience—remains what it is, the outcome (C) rests on B.

My friend, cardiologist Robert Eliot, MD, told me this story, which I think perfectly illustrates the ABC principle. Many years ago, Bob was lecturing in Riyadh, Saudi Arabia, and had some time on his hands, so he decided to take a walk around the town with an interpreter. As the two men stood on a street corner waiting for the light to change, two stretch Mercedes limos came barreling through the intersection and collided head-on. The first thing Bob thought was, *This is going to be interesting. I'll get to see a mini-version of the Arab-Arab war played out right here on the street.* Instead, he watched as the two passengers got out of their respective vehicles, examined the damage, and approached one another quite cordially. They even smiled as they began to converse. Bob asked the interpreter what in the world was going on, and he replied, "You see, sir, they are observing that everything that happens is the will of Allah. And they're saying to each other, 'Isn't it wonderful that God has arranged for us to meet?'"

This example illustrates how each of us sees things differently. Therefore, we will each interpret what we experience differently. People like Phyllis, who interpret situations as hopeless, are down more often than not. Others, like Kate—and to a growing degree, Lauren—experience more positive emotions and thus can see things in an optimistic light. In Kate's case, had she not been an optimist, she might have believed that her life was lessened because her boyfriend left her. But she never believed that, not for one moment.

Tools to Help You Move On

When a relationship is over, it stings, and it's frightening because you don't know what lies ahead. The good news is that what happens from there on is up to you. If you want to be happy, let go of the belief that you are nothing without him and take on the attitude that *you are and can be what you choose to be* without him. In fact, let's just leave *him* out of the sentence altogether. Now it reads: You are and can be what you choose to be. So choose to be independent. Choose to be strong. Choose to be happy.

The following tools will help you do just that.

Lead with Your Strengths

What someone who has been rejected needs is a quick shot of self-confidence, and you won't find that trying to fix what you think you're doing wrong. Positive psychologists consider that a waste of valuable time. Research has shown that only one of every three people who go the traditional clinical psychology route (in which therapists help patients identify and correct weaknesses) improve with therapy.

It's far better to go the positive psychology route, which proposes that you seek out the things you do right and well and try to do them even better. In other words, identify your strengths and then lead your life from them.

Everyone has strengths. Your strengths act as ultimate buffers against negative situations. They are defined as the abilities, assets, or qualities you have, can use, and get joy from. If you understand what your strengths are, you can expand on them and call them up in times of need. This is part of the theory called broaden and build, put forth by Barbara Frederickson, PhD, a positive psychologist at the University of North Carolina at Chapel Hill.

I can almost hear you thinking, *Strengths? What does he mean by strengths? How do I know what my strengths are?*

You're not alone if you don't have a clue how to identify your strengths. Most women don't know themselves well enough to determine what their special qualities are. One of my coauthors was such a person. I knew recognized strengths right away (okay, it did take me 11 years of schooling to learn how to assess them), but she needed to find them for herself. Rather than telling her outright, I engaged her in a dialogue just as I would any person I'm counseling.

Ina: Okay, Dan. I want to know what my strengths are and how to use them. Now what?

Dan: Ina, tell me about a time in your life when you engaged in an activity for which you had joy and pride both during the process and as a result of it.

Ina: When I'm writing.

Dan: Fine. Tell me about one of those times connected to your writing that's particularly pronounced in your recollection.

Ina: It was with my first book, when I learned a publisher had accepted it.

Dan: And what was the nature of that book?

Ina: It taught the layperson how to understand the basics of open-heart surgery.

Dan: What made that book stand out in your recollection?

Ina: It was my first published book. Before that, I never thought I was really a writer.

Dan: It confirmed that you were really good at something that you loved anyhow.

Ina: That's right.

Dan: How did being a published author change you as a person?

Ina: My self-esteem went off the charts.

Dan: So it's the first time that you confirmed to yourself that you actually had real talent.

Ina: Yes.

Dan: What did you do with that talent?

Ina: I wrote another book.

Dan: So you went out and built on your talent. And in the process of writing that second book, what did you learn about yourself?

Ina: That I could do just about anything I really put my mind to.

Dan: So not only did you learn that you were a talented writer, you learned that you could achieve things that earlier in your life you could only dream of. Once you became aware that you could transform your dreams into reality, what did that mean to the quality of your life?

Ina: It showed me that there was something I could do in this world without help from anybody else.

Dan: So you believed in yourself. That's a strength. By writing a second book, you showed perseverance. Perseverance is a strength. By keeping an open mind and going out and developing research for your books, you developed a broader knowledge base, so you're a scholar, a researcher, and an interviewer. Those are strengths. I've already identified many of your strengths in just a short period of time.

Ina: Anything else?

Dan: Yes. How do you feel when you go to sleep at night having completed a great paragraph or a great page that day?

Ina: I feel great because I have something tangible that was not there when I woke up that morning.

Dan: So you actually engaged in the act of creation. If you can do that with frequency, at the end of your life, what are you going to be able to say about your life?

Ina: That it had meaning.

Dan: Yes. For you and for people you've never met. Just by your writing, you touched people in ways that make their lives better. So altruism: caring about people you'll never know. That's a strength, too.

You can do this same exercise without a dialogue, of course. Just recall a time, an event, or an experience when life was good for you. (It can be comparatively good—it doesn't have to be great.) Then take out a pencil and paper and write down the answers to these questions.

- What were the circumstances of that experience? That is, how did it happen?
- Who was responsible for the experience?
- How did you feel during the experience?
- What part of the experience made you feel that way?
- What information about yourself can you take away from the experience?

Make a Commitment to Yourself

I can't tell you how many women I've met who have abandoned themselves and don't have a clue that they've done it. If you want to be your own best friend, here's how.

Think about the best friendship you ever had and what you did to make that friendship so good. I can guess your answers: "I paid attention to the other person. I listened to them. I interacted in a loving, caring, nurturing, meaningful way." Yes, yes, yes to all three. You pay attention because you want the other person to love you and be there for you if ever you need them—just as you would be there for them, under any conditions. You are secure in having a best friend you can count on.

Well, what if you paid a little more attention to yourself *in that same way*? As a matter of course, you ask your friends how they feel, how their day was, what's happening in their lives. Why not ask the same questions of yourself? Ask what's going on with your body, mind, and spirit. Ask what you need to nurture your body today, to nurture your mind. What energy, time, and resources do you need to invest? How can you make yourself feel as good as you try to make your best friend feel?

Nurture Your Passion

George Burns was fond of saying that every day, you should do at least one thing you love.

Maybe you don't love your job, which is useful for making a living and paying the bills, but that doesn't preclude you from writing those two or three pages or listening to a symphony. It doesn't mean you can't take a walk in the park and admire the beauty of the season.

None of those things cost anything, and they feed your soul. And that's what people are looking for, really. We're mistaken when we believe that material things feed our souls. What they do is create excitement.

Here's a personal example. I love my grandchildren. I don't interact with them every day, but I do think of them every day. I get a lot of pleasure and happiness just thinking about them. Then when I'm with them, I have this huge foundation to build upon to have real experiences, and I build memories from those visits that enlarge those resources even more.

Put Meaning into Your Life

Meaning is the end result of purpose. Meaning is the payoff for living a purposeful life. What is it we want to be known for in the end? If I said to you, "Let's put two lines on your headstone about your professional life, but there won't be any room left for anything about your being a wife or mother or grandmother," would you go for that? Of course not. Very few of the women I know would want any part of that. The other is more important. Meaning is what we center our lives around. It is core to our reason for being. But you need to know first what is meaningful to you. If you don't know where you're going, you're not likely to get there. (Or as Yogi Berra said, "If you don't know where you're going, you're going to be lost when you get there.") And that's where intention comes in.

What is intention? If you said, "I intend to write a book," that's an example. That's something you can work on. Intention is the determination that leads to an outcome. It generally requires certain steps to get there, and each of the steps also has a certain outcome. If the outcome isn't what we expect, we make changes along the way. And we try again.

Intention will give you a roadmap to engage in your world meaningfully, so intend to do something specific—the more specific the better. You decide to have a family event. You have to call everybody. You have to get a date when the schedules line up. You have to find the place you're going to meet. You have to ask everyone when it's a good time for them to come. And on and on. Intention is a desire to do something of significance with a direction and the resources to carry it out.

In short, get involved. Every happy woman we interviewed for this book is proactive. Proactivity equals intention. If you want to get over a bad relationship or believing you're nothing without "him," make a plan and act on it. That's what intention is all about.

Being in your own life is everything. Being responsible for yourself, being there for yourself, listening to yourself, nurturing yourself, and engaging yourself so that you can go out and do things for other people whom you value. You may be without a man, but you're certainly not "nothing." Sure, there are scary parts along the way, but none are so fearsome that you can't overcome them, particularly if you commit yourself to doing what it takes to live a beautiful, fulfilling life.

And why wouldn't you?

CHAPTER SEVEN

Circling the Career Track

Some of us are becoming the men we wanted to marry.
Gloria Steinem

Work can be separated into three categories, some or all of which may at some point overlap. There is a *job*, which is essentially what you do to earn a living. There is a *career*, which is about advancing yourself and contributing to the betterment of something about which you hopefully care very deeply. And then there is a *calling*. A calling is work in which you find great meaning. Mother Teresa had a calling of the highest level. So did T. E. Lawrence (of Arabia) and Mahatma Gandhi. The difference between a career and a calling is that people who follow a calling can commit their working lives to remarkably difficult work that might burn others out in a matter of months, yet they still find joy in it.

This chapter addresses the issues of women and careers and the ways those careers impact on happiness. We will also look at the career *traps* women fall into, presumably on their way to the top. Most career women can't imagine their lives without their work. A career can provide financial independence and a sense of purpose, nurture confidence, and in many cases, come with benefits such as health care, educational support, and retirement funds. Beyond that, women have accomplished and do accomplish amazing things in the course of their working lives. Of course, though, it's not all a bed of roses (no one gets to be happy all the time, remember).

In this chapter, we'll look at how career problems develop and can sometimes become happiness traps to be avoided. Ironically, the problems women most commonly associate with their careers become greater the more successful they become. For example, it's when they're successful at climbing the first few rungs on the career ladder that they're faced with the big work/life questions: "How do I find and keep the right guy when I'm making twice as much as I'd imagined I could make at this age? Do I stop working to start a family? If I stop, will I ever go back? When I go back, will they remember who I am? Will the person who fills in for me while I'm on maternity leave be better, smarter, and quicker than I am? Am I getting too old to be considered for promotion?"

I've heard them all, and what I've noticed is that when these questions arise—and women mishandle them—they can quickly turn a flourishing career track into a career trap.

Once Upon a Time

Today's woman is very lucky, *or so she has been told*. She can absolutely have it all: a glorious career, monetary success, happy children, a caring partner, loyal friends, and an incredibly busy social life.

Well, I'd sure like to meet the person who sold her that bill of goods. I wonder how many hours she has in *her* day.

The reality is, if you're trying to do and to be all these things, you're going to struggle for the rest of your life because it's never going to happen. Like perfectionism, having it all is an illusion. And if your expectations are

What Happy Women Know

that this is a reality, I can almost guarantee that every time you find yourself lacking in one or another area, you're going to blame yourself.

But don't.

Because if you're guilty of anything at all, it's buying into this late 20th century fairy tale. And why wouldn't you want to believe it? Who doesn't want to have it all?

The 1950s were a time when life was much simpler. You had only to flip on your television set to get a true reflection of American culture at its best. Remember how Jane Wyatt practically floated to the door to welcome her husband home in *Father Knows Best?* Perfectly turned out, in a spotless house, with a four-course meal ready and waiting. Or how about cheery Barbara Billingsley, aka June Cleaver, always with a smile, always happy to take a backseat to her three "boys"—Wally, Beaver, and Mr. Cleaver?

Would Jane or Barbara's screen characters ever *think* of leaving the home for a career in law or business? There was about as much chance of that as there was of Lucy and Ethel becoming investment bankers.

(Okay, I admit that, yes, the real Jane and Barbara did leave the house to go to work at the studio, but let's file that under exceptions to the rule.)

I'm guessing, but I would say that the majority of women who worked in the 1950s and earlier did so as clerks, secretaries, teachers, or nurses, because that's what "girls" did. Be sure to have something to "fall back on" is what they were told, in case life didn't go according to plan. All of which was the nice way of saying, "If for some reason you never get married, if (heaven forbid!) you have to *rely on yourself financially,* you can always make a living."

Let's return to television shows, because I think nothing mirrors the attitudes of the times like the day's most popular shows. In the 1960s, Mary Tyler Moore played Rob's wife and Richie's mother on *The Dick van Dyke Show.* A decade later, she was handed the plum role of single, angst-filled TV producer Mary Richards on *The Mary Tyler Moore Show.* It was one giant leap for womankind. In the 1980s, we watched Candice Bergen play the fiercely independent (and notably unmarried) Murphy Brown, a character who almost lost her job when she became pregnant and chose to have the baby. During the same era, Phylicia Rashad was Clair Huxtable, a lawyer and mother of three on *The Cosby Show*. Yes, women with careers did become cultural icons and role models for young girls as women took on greater and greater importance in the workplace.

Even Mattel's Barbie got into the career act. In 1965, Barbie was an astronaut. She went to medical school somewhere along the way, and in 1973 there was Barbie the surgeon, soon to be followed by Barbie the NASCAR driver and Barbie the diplomat. (We're still awaiting Mommy Barbie; it will come.)

What happened in those 45 years to bring us from point A to point B was the blossoming of the women's movement. The seeds of this movement took root in 1960—around the time the FDA approved the birth control pill—and coalesced in 1963 with the publication of Betty Freidan's runaway bestseller, *The Feminine Mystique*. In it, Freidan gave voice to millions of her sisters when she wrote:

> If I am right, the problem that has no name stirring in the minds of so many American women today is not a matter of loss of femininity or too much education, or the demands of domesticity. It is far more important than anyone recognizes . . . it may well be the key to our future as a nation and a culture. We can no longer ignore that voice within women that says, "I want something more than my husband and my children and my home."

The reason it took so long, Freidan tells us, was that the early Mrs. Everywoman struggled alone. As she plodded through domestic chores, from feeding the kids balanced meals to endless trips back and forth to

A TIMELINE OF THE WOMEN'S MOVEMENT

1957 The number of women and men voting is approximately equal for the first time.

1960 The FDA approves oral contraceptives. While feminist sentiment had been around for centuries, it was the Pill that helped transform a feeling into a movement.

1963 Betty Freidan's bestseller, *The Feminine Mystique,* is published, attacking the popular notion that women could find fulfillment only through childbearing and homemaking.

1964 Title VII of the Civil Rights Act bars employment discrimination by private employers, employment agencies, and unions based on race, sex, and other grounds.

1966 Twenty-eight women found the National Organization for Women to function as a civil rights organization for women.

1968 The National Abortion Rights Action League (NARAL) is founded.

1970 Women's wages fall to 59 cents for every dollar earned by men. The Equal Rights Amendment is reintroduced into Congress.

1973 In Roe v. Wade, the Supreme Court establishes a woman's right to abortion, effectively canceling the anti-abortion laws of 46 states.

1978 For the first time in history, more women than men enter college.

1981 Sandra Day O'Connor is the first woman to be appointed to the US Supreme Court. In 1993, Ruth Bader Ginsberg joins her.

2007 Hillary Rodham Clinton announces that she will run for the office of president of the United States.

after-school activities, she had no one to ask about the possibility of a life beyond her role as helpmate—no one but herself.

By the mid-1980s, the stage was set for the first generation of women to expect a working life much like a man's. Unlike Rosie the Riveter, who during World War II went to work in the factory as her man left for battle and just as quickly gave up the position when he came home from the war, the women of the 1980s anticipated having decades-long, fulfilling careers. Prescient designers Donna Karan and Calvin Klein fashioned women's suits in blue pinstripes, and soon all of Seventh Avenue followed their lead. *Ms.* magazine, with Gloria Steinem at the helm, became the career woman's bible. Courses in women's studies sprang up on college campuses across the country, and skirted legs were being crossed under tables in some of the most influential boardrooms in corporate America.

Many young women who married during this period—including those who had been told to be teachers and secretaries—could be found tucking their babies into bed and heading down to the living room to study for the Medical College Admission Tests (MCATs). (It might interest you to know that in 1873, when women were first entering universities in this country, Edward Clarke, MD, of Harvard Medical School published a book entitled *Sex in Education: Or, a Fair Chance for Girls.* In it, he contended that for their own good, women should not be allowed in colleges or universities because the cognitive demands on their brains would somehow atrophy their reproductive organs.)

Suddenly business schools, medical schools, law schools, and even rabbinical schools were flooded with applications. Happiness, it seemed, was only a postage stamp away.

In the latter part of the 20th century, as American culture elevated work to priority number one, bright, aspiring women discovered opportunities open to them at every turn. "You *can* have it all!" they were told—marriage, a career, children, and a full, fulfilling life. How could they not heed the clarion call?

For many women, a most important goal, if not the *only* goal, became career success. Marriage and children could wait. Career replaced family. The job was all.

But was it?

As work wheedled its way into the core of women's consciousness, untold numbers were quickly caught up in the intensity of this new perspective, even despite the fact that the opportunities open to men were barely as accessible to women. Women had to fight long and hard—in fact, they had to fight many times harder to break through "the glass ceiling." It wasn't enough to be as smart as the guy in the next office; women had to be two times, three times, five times brighter and harder working. For every two steps it took a man to advance his career, it took a woman five.

Where was the equality?

What equality? demanded Texas governor Ann Richards in a widely published speech. Women are *far* more capable, she claimed, before backing up her statement with Faith Whittlesey's now famous line: "Remember, Ginger Rogers did everything Fred Astaire did, but she did it backward and in high heels."

It's a Choice, So Choose

Around the late 1990s, as the euphoria settled down, reality set in, and with it, a few basic problems began to emerge. Career success didn't necessarily bring the happiness it promised, and when it did, that happiness often came at a cost.

Searching for "Mr. Right"

Judith, a 35-year-old investment banker who reminded me of a young Annette Bening, settled herself into the straight-backed chair across from my desk. She had come to the ranch for a week to wind down, but from the way she fidgeted in her chair and nervously played with the paperweight on my desk, I got the sense that sitting still was not her forte. She probably would have been much happier in the middle of a thorny merger and acquisition.

We started talking, and within the first few minutes, she let me know precisely what was on her mind. It wasn't an uncommon dilemma for a woman in her position. "I'm making several hundred thousand dollars a year, Dr. Baker, with perks like you wouldn't believe." She tossed this off as nonchalantly as if she were saying, "Nice weather we're having, isn't it?"

I responded, quite naturally, "And the problem is?"

She told me she holds a position of greater status and power than the majority of men she meets. They don't earn nearly what she does, and she thinks she's scaring them off. "My first marriage suffered from the same money problem. Early on, I landed a position with my company that boosted my earnings up to twice his. Instead of being pleased for both of us, he started controlling my spending—even though I was using mostly my money. He even suggested that I quit. I found myself sneaking money from my own account just to buy a new suit he thought I didn't really need. The marriage lasted 2 years, and I blame its demise on my salary."

Strange as it sounds, she may be right. According to the US Bureau of Labor Statistics, in 2006, about a third of all working women in the United States earned more money than their husbands. That number is trending upward, and it's expected to keep going as more families include two wage earners, and women are as well educated and as qualified as men for any given job.

"I want to meet someone I can have fun with," she continued. "Someone I can relate to. But if I find a guy who looks like a possibility, I feel like I have to walk on eggshells. I don't want him to see my apartment because it's probably nicer than his. And I don't want to discuss my work because I'm afraid to emasculate him. You know men and their egos."

I do.

"What specifically do you want?" I asked her.

"I want a life. I want a husband *and* my 2.5 children *and* my career. Women do it all the time. Is that so much to ask for?"

> Happy women know that before taking one more step up
> the career ladder, it's wise to know who and what is
> supporting that ladder and where that step is taking them.

When I meet a woman like Judith—that is, someone with an established career who is keen to find a partner and have a family—the first thing I want to be certain of is that she has a solid, healthy relationship with herself, because that's going to give her the best chance of attracting a decent prospective partner. The minute a woman is seen to be needy or vulnerable—I don't care if she's CEO, CFO, or sole owner of World Wide Wickets—she's going to be a magnet for the wrong type of guy.

"You're lucky," I said. "You have options—and I'm not referring to the stock kind."

I suggested that if she wants to keep the balance of power on an even keel, her best chance is to find a very mature and together man or one with comparable or greater resources—or someone who cares little about all those trappings. There are plenty of men like that out there, I assured her. I know quite a few men who earn far less than their wives, and it has never been an issue. I also know some men who are happy to be "househusbands," and they, too, are self-assured and not threatened at all.

Of course, the next step was finding a way to meet them. I encouraged Judith to think carefully about where she might meet someone who holds similar values to hers. "If you want to catch a sailfish, you don't go into the pond in your backyard. You go where the big fish are," I said. I suggested that she become more deeply involved in organizations and activities that interest her, where she might have a better chance of meeting a partner than she would commuting to the office. "Join a political party," I told her. "Get involved in the symphony board, join a running or cycling club. Get involved in something you care about."

Then we discussed the "fix-up," and she groaned. "I've done that. You can't even imagine how awful that can be."

"Then maybe you need to look for a matchmaker who knows you better, someone who is smart enough to see common ground on which a relationship could develop." This time her groan was followed by a sigh as she agreed to try again.

> Happy women know that if you're looking for someone to share your life—including your career—you have to be proactive, and you can't compromise yourself. If you try to make your partner bigger by making yourself smaller, the relationship won't work.

There was a scene in the movie *When Harry Met Sally* where Meg Ryan's Sally cries, "I drove him away, and I'm about to be 40!" The writer, Nora Ephron, crafted that line after the 1986 *Newsweek* magazine cover story that stated in so many words that *a 40-year-old single, college-educated woman was more likely to be killed by a terrorist than to get married.* It was an article that I'm certain struck terror in the hearts of just about every single woman, whether she wanted to admit it or not. This social panic became the central plot theme of almost every episode of HBO's *Sex and the City* throughout its run.

Rebuttals were crafted and speeches delivered to refute that claim, but it took more than 10 years before statistics were gathered to show how erroneous the interpretation was and another 10 before *Newsweek* retracted it with the cover statement on June 6, 2006: *We Were Wrong!* It seems the original article was based on a study entitled "Marriage Patterns in the United States," which was written by Harvard-Yale social scientists David

Bloom, Neil Bennett, and Patricia Craig. Embedded in the study were statistics that showed the following: Women tended to marry guys 2 or 3 years older. During the baby boom, with each passing year, an increasing number of babies were born, meaning that in 1955, there were more babies than in 1953. So women born in 1955 who were looking for men 2 years older—baby boys born in 1953—faced more competition. (Sounds like the same scarcity of resources our foremothers faced, doesn't it?)

What finally happened to those baby-boomer women who were in fact 40 and not married? It turns out that most of them did get married or will eventually. A study published in 2004 by Princeton sociologists Joshua Goldstein, PhD, and Catherine Kenney, PhD, predicted that 90 percent of baby-boomer women will eventually marry at some point in their lives.

A Baby? Maybe

Okay, let's assume your career is in high gear, you've found Mr. Right, and you've married him. Here comes the next fastball: Do you go for the family? Is biology heading for a showdown with your career plans, or can you wait another year? When do you reach that threshold when you say, "Oh, my God, if I'm going to do this, I'd better get to it."

Many women fear missing out on the profoundly rewarding experience of being a mother, hence the push/pull—the "should I or shouldn't I" dilemma that can make life exceedingly difficult. Fertility clinics make fortunes by catering to frantic women who wake up to the ticking of their biological clocks at the 11½th hour. Fortunately these clinics can help many of them to reverse time.

I met Andrea, a divorce specialist and the daughter of a friend, at an outdoor luncheon one afternoon last summer. At 41, she had just made partner in a large Phoenix law firm. We were talking about the joys of her new partnership when she suddenly started backpedaling. "Yes, it's great and all. But to be honest, it has its drawbacks."

"Yes? In what way?" I asked.

"Recently I went to visit a friend in the hospital, and I passed the nursery and all those beautiful babies and beaming parents, and I realized that I may just have gone past my optimal level of fertility. I'm scared I'm never going to hold my own baby. Or that I'm never going to take my child by the hand and hold it tight when he goes in for the first day of school."

Postponing having children so as not to interfere with a career is one of the career traps women have faced for years. Andrea is just one of many women I've met who has developed so much momentum on the career track that she worries she may have blown right through her reproductive shelf life.

What Happy Moms Know

Now let's say you and Mr. Right have decided to have a baby. You take 3 months' maternity leave. You fall hopelessly in love with your baby, and lucky you—you can afford to stay home with her if you want. Here comes your *next* dilemma. Do you go back to work, or do you put your career on hold for the next 10 years despite the time, effort, and yes, money you invested in getting your Stanford MBA? Research shows the longer you remain out of the job market, the harder it is to pick up where you left off, so it's a serious decision with far-reaching effects. But that may not even be the issue. Try this one on for size: Are you willing to let someone else watch your baby take her first step or kiss her scraped knee when she falls from the slide?

A Work Life That Works for You

The "mommy track" seems to split off in many different directions as women and their employers become more creative about ways to keep women in the workplace. For example, one of the women we interviewed for this book abruptly gave up her career to move to the suburbs, get married, and have children. As her children got older, she chose to combine work and mothering on her terms, accepting only those freelance projects she believed she could handle without compromising time spent with her family. Other women take part in job sharing, work from home, or far less often, take their babies with them to work.

There are also women who relinquish their careers altogether in favor of staying at home to care for the children, at least while they're small. That choice, it turns out, isn't always as easy as the moms expect.

I once attended a seminar where I listened to women talk about this very subject. I'll never forget one whose story encapsulated the dilemma of many working moms I've counseled. The speaker was a middle manager at a pharmaceutical company, where she'd worked since graduating from college. Now, 11 years later, she was going cold turkey—quitting her job to stay home with her 2-year-old son. At first, she told the audience, she felt as if she had fallen into some kind of foreign world—a world that was filled with high-pitched voices and smelled like a mixture of wax crayons and chicken fingers. She said she confused the words *play date* and *play dough* and learned the hard way that cranberry juice comes in boxes. And she told us that the first time she faced a form that asked for her occupation, she had to think long and hard about how to reply.

She missed her work friends and wearing something other than sweats every day, but in the end, the tradeoff was "magnificent." She said, "I can't imagine not being there to see the look on the face of my Little Leaguer the day he got his first hit, or watching my 6-year-old daughter play the role of a teapot in her first-grade play."

Happy women know that with each phase of life, they give up something, but they also get something in return.

In October 2006, the *New York Times* reported on a study showing that despite the rush of women into the workplace, "mothers are spending at least as much time with their children today as they did 40 years ago, and the amount of child care and housework performed by fathers has sharply increased." This statistic came from an analysis of thousands of personal diaries, was reported in a book called *Changing Rhythms of American Family Life,* and was based on a study done by Suzanne Bianchi, PhD, a sociologist at the University of Maryland. The data also showed that married and single parents spent more time teaching, playing with, and caring for their children than parents did 40 years ago.

As the hours mothers spent with their children went up, their hours of housework declined. It appears that spending time with the children has taken on the highest priority.

There are also countless women who, even if they wanted to, can't *afford* to leave their jobs to raise the children—particularly today, when it takes two paychecks just to make ends meet and still have a little left over for a box of crayons. I truly believe many of them would gladly welcome the opportunity to trade places with the woman who spoke at that seminar.

Clearly, there is no one right way to combine work and family life, only the way that's right for you. Ask yourself which combination does the best job of meeting *most* of your needs. Sometimes you're weighing apples and oranges. If you go this way, you have more family time but less income. If you go that way, you have more income but don't see your family enough. Or if you go this way, you make a lot of money, but you're not doing what you love, and if you do what you love, you may fall short on being able to buy the things you want your children to have. Life will always present some difficult decisions. We didn't leave them behind on the Savannah; they've just reached a higher level and become more abstract.

Aging Ain't What It Used to Be

I hate to bring this up, but it's a fact of life. We've seen what happens when women start racing against the biological clock in an effort to start a family before it's too late. But that's not the only career issue related to the passage of time. There's another one, affectionately called *getting older*. I bring up this issue with a raised consciousness and 20 years of experience with women executives. Age discrimination is very real—you know it and I know it.

A junior executive in her twenties with an eye toward a managerial position or perhaps making partner in her firm often makes an effort to look a little older than she is, just to give herself some credibility in the boardroom. But when she hits her forties, watch how quickly she throws that strategy into reverse. Now she finds herself in a meeting sizing up the 20- and 30-somethings and calling her dermatologist or plastic surgeon at the first sign of a new wrinkle.

Here's where the "no justice" part comes in: While some career-focused women want to look youthful as long as they can, their male counterparts—for the most part—seem to coast through sixtydom with nary a worry, at least about how their age affects their employment status. There are plenty of powerhouses in their seventies and eighties who are proud of every year. Sumner Redstone, Rupert Murdoch, Si Newhouse, Warren Buffet, and Jack Welch come to mind, and I'm certain there are many, many more.

I'm the first in line to say there's nothing wrong with doing whatever it takes to make you healthier and more attractive, but I do have trouble with the concept of women undergoing surgery for the sake of *looking younger for the job.* Studies tell me I'm way outnumbered. The American Society for Aesthetic Plastic Surgery reports that surgical and nonsurgical cosmetic procedures increased by 44 percent from 2003 to 2004, to a total of almost 11.9 million. Ninety percent of these procedures were performed on women.

When the results of surgery meet the patient's expectations, she can feel very good about it. But surgery has its limits, and I'm always concerned about how a woman will cope when surgery can no longer make a significant difference. Will she develop the mindset and emotional framework to deal with the natural process of aging? Or will she be frustrated by something over which she has no control?

I wouldn't relive my teen years for anything. Would I love to have the *energy* I had as a teenager? You bet. Would I want to be as naive and ignorant as I was back then? Not a chance. I paid too many dues and too much tuition to get where I am. So yes, there is a vast difference between men and women when it comes to vanity, for all the reasons discussed in Chapter 2. And I ask you to remember that women's insecurities stem from fear raising its ugly head again: Women never believe they are enough. I suspect that even if I talk until I'm blue in the face, this fact will continue to stare us down.

Believing Your Job Is Your Identity

The second most commonly asked question when two people meet is "What do you do?" (The first is "What is your name?") That says a lot about America's cultural consciousness because Americans tend to rank people when they meet them. Although it probably shouldn't, the answer to the question "What do you do?" tells much about who you are. If I told you I was a garbage collector, chances are your reaction would be different than if I told you I was a neurosurgeon at the Mayo Clinic.

Another problem can easily arise when who you are and what you do are too closely linked because when you no longer do it, where are you? A blurred line between job and identity is one of the reasons so many people hesitate to retire—or are blindsided by the reality of life beyond the corporate office. It doesn't matter whether you're moving into retirement from the executive suite or the classroom, if you once spent your days as a CEO, a secretary, or a teacher. People fear leaving their jobs because they have nothing to go *to*. They get trapped. Even though they're tired and don't want to work any more, they stay on.

> Happy women know that part of their identity
> is tied to what they do, but they never let what they do
> become their whole identity.

If the trap is becoming one-dimensional with regard to work, the tool that springs you is the diversified life.

Think of your life as an investment portfolio. If you had gone to your broker and he told you to invest everything you own in this great stock called Enron, and you had listened, where would you be today? Pretty unhappy is my guess. But if he instead encouraged you to look at 10 different options he believed were going to do well and was right about 7, you would be one happy camper.

You can't be just mom, chauffeur, and wife, professional or executive. Your goal is to achieve a life that's more like a mosaic or a symphony you compose with your interests and strengths. In Western culture, careers provide us with meaning and a sense of purpose, but your career is not your life. Remember Phyllis, who completely lost her identity as Mrs. Doctor when her husband the surgeon flew the coop? Phyllis was the poster child for one-dimensional living. Had she been active in church, community, or a cause or nurtured more friendships or family relationships, she wouldn't have been stuck trying to build a life from the ground up when Alan decided to blow out of there.

Your career can be all sorts of things, but unless you want the career track to be the career *trap,* it cannot be your sole identity.

How Happy Are You at Work?

If you're putting in 40-hour workweeks, that's 2,080 working hours per year—and who among us does *just* that? But okay, let's say that's the case. Do you enjoy those 2,080 hours? Let's rephrase that a bit. Do you enjoy *most* of those hours? You do if you are engaged in a career that dovetails with what's important to you, and that happiness will surely carry over to the rest of your life.

Now ask yourself what's important to you and what that has to do with your work. For example, if you value learning, honesty, and friendship, it's important to be in a position that offers them to you. You need to—and indeed have a right to—feel good about your work. The cost of ignoring that need is low self-esteem, weakened health, and disruption in your relationships.

You also have a right to a life outside the office. If it turns out that your work *is* your life, you may need to change a few things. I'm not talking about a major overhaul but rather a gradual redesign, one that employs two of the principles we've already discussed: Kaizen, the Japanese method of continual improvement through small incremental steps, and the 60-minute hour principle, which says there are only 60 minutes in each hour, and it's up to you how you slice them up. I suggest committing as many minutes as you're able to the things you can feel good about.

First, try to destress yourself. Being tightly wound affects your performance at work and becomes a self-perpetuating cycle. Whenever you feel yourself tightening up, find a quiet place where you can sit by yourself, close your eyes, and for 5 minutes, either meditate or practice deep breathing. Make it a regular part of your day and do it several times a day. If you have only 3 minutes, use them. Eventually, those minutes will add up, and you'll find that a certain sense of calm comes over you.

The second tool is similar but broader. Let's say you're working a 60-hour week. Try cutting back by 5 hours the first week and then consciously plan what you're going to do with that time. You can spend it on your health or your relationships or doing a service, such as reading to someone who would welcome the companionship. The next week, try to do it again, and maybe make it 5½ hours. Continue with small, doable changes that lead to slightly bigger ones.

Work and Life: A Fine Balance

Career. Romance. Family. Can you have them all?

Why not?

What you need to think about is how each fits best into your life and what it will take to make you happy. If you're not sure about the balance that will do that, here's another tool to put to good use. I call it the sinking boat analogy, and people who come to see me find it very helpful in determining what's really important to them.

Let's say you tell me, "I'm having trouble choosing between my career, my child, and taking care of myself." Here's what I'd say: "Think of the things in your life that are most meaningful to you—in addition to family and friends—and turn them into people. For example, make your health a person and your career a person. Imagine all these 'people' are with you in a rowboat, on a lake. But somewhere in the middle of the lake, the boat springs a leak and starts sinking. You can save yourself and only one of the passengers, and you have to swim quite a distance to shore to get that person to safety. Which 'person' do you save?"

Of course, you'll choose the child. Now imagine that once you've brought her to shore, you look out and see the other "people" still bobbing up and down, and you realize there's a chance you can save one more, but you're sure you can't save all of them. So you swim desperately, and which one do you retrieve next? Your health, probably.

This is a forced-choice priority exercise, but it shows you what's important, and then you can decide how much of your life you want to devote to each. So maybe the baby doesn't get 100 percent of you, but she gets 51 percent. Then health gets 20 percent, work gets 5 percent, your husband gets 20 percent, and friends get 4 percent. Try it and see what happens. You'll be quite surprised at how well this works.

No matter how near or far you are from the executive suite, as you approach the top, the pull between work and life seems to be more difficult for women than for men. But an increasing number of women have help from their husbands, who are more than happy to stay at home to raise the children or who work from home. This type of arrangement works well for many of today's women executives and at least one highly successful cosmetic dermatologist. She works in Miami and lectures around the world while her husband plays the major role in caring for their young children. He is far from alone. The number of stay-at-home fathers increased by 50 percent between 2003 and 2004, according to an analysis of the data at www.rebeldad.com, a blog for this particular population.

All in all, I think today's women are becoming more comfortable with the choices they're making in terms of balancing their lives. Knowing full well that it is no longer an either/or situation—meaning the position of chief of surgery or a personal life—women have reached a point in their careers where they are willing to accept that they can go only so far and so high and make only so much money and still be a "success." The important thing is to decide what kind of success you want to be and at what point in your life.

> Happy women know that you *can* have it all,
> just not all at the same time.

I truly hope that this generation of school-age girls is looking at their mothers and saying, "I don't want to give up anything! I'm going to craft my life in a way that allows me to have what I want. I might not have it all at the same time, but if I take it in steps, I can have it in a way that's successful for me."

Some women will choose to devote themselves to a career early on and then pause it, have their children, and come back and pick up where they left off. Others will figure out how to build a support system around their children and accept that they may have to give up some of the childrearing control. Still others may choose to give up control over the pace of their career.

The key is recognizing what you can give up and what you need to keep. Today's career woman realizes that adding value to her life means delegating those things that don't add value to it. And that's different for each woman, too. While the generation before them had some guilt about not picking up the dry cleaning or not making the meals or not—as Bonnie Fuller, editorial director at American Media and the mother of four, so aptly put it in her book *The Joys of Much Too Much*—"having an organized sock drawer," this generation's woman seems to be perfectly okay with the nanny doing laundry and with ordering takeout meals. She chooses what she's going to throw herself at with abandon, and that's more than good enough—that's success in the truest sense.

CHAPTER EIGHT

Transcending Loss

If we had no winter, the spring would not be so pleasant.
Anne Bradstreet

You cannot be human alone. So says author Robert Bly in his book *The Sibling Society.*

We are by our very natures prone to seek someone, and more often many people, to love. Love can enter our hearts at any time and any age. Sometimes it strikes when we least expect it, such as on a subway or across the proverbial crowded room. Sometimes it even begins with the faintest of sounds, such as when you hear the heartbeat of your unborn baby for the first time.

As we begin to love, we bond closer and closer with the object of our love. That too is nature's way. Attraction, connection, falling in love, and ultimately bonding are absolutely essential for the survival of the human race.

But love can also lead to one of life's great paradoxes, for just as the moment of conception assures that death will follow, the moment we learn to love or become attached, we must be prepared to one day lose our loved one—be it a parent, a spouse, a child, a dear friend, or a pet. Losses come in other forms as well. We may lose a marriage; a job; our health; or unmet hopes, dreams, or desires.

You may wonder why we've included a chapter on loss in this book about happiness. It's because no matter how happy our lives may be, we all will experience personal losses. When that happens, grief is inevitable. But those losses don't have to set the tone for the rest of our lives. The question is, do we grieve in a healthy way and move on, or do we entrap ourselves in an unhealthy way?

Happy women know that grief in itself is not a trap.
Believing that you can never transcend it is.

Learning to grieve in a healthy way is what this chapter is all about.

The Price of Love

All questions have implicit direction, and sometimes, without our realizing it, our questions lead us down counterproductive paths. When we ask "Why me?" that is really only part of what we want to know. The larger question is: "Why did the universe choose to visit this misfortune on me?" When my son Ryan died in my arms of hyaline membrane disease, my very first question was "Why?" The doctors talked to me about the undeveloped alveoli in his lungs and his inability to process oxygen, and yes, by the time they were through, I understood the physiological processes that led to his death. But it wasn't the physical process I wrestled with. What I wanted to know was why it had to happen at all. And frankly, there is no answer to that question, or at least no satisfactory answer. It's the price of love.

Rabbi Harold Kushner's *When Bad Things Happen to Good People* addresses this same issue. Rabbi Kushner, who wrote the book after the early death of his son, reasoned it like this: "If I'm a good person, then I have an implicit contract with the power of the universe. I have been good, so why this immense sadness and grief?" It's the story of Job all over again.

Another rabbi I know tells a corollary story. A woman came to his study and announced, "I can no longer believe in God." The rabbi wondered why, as he knew she was a fairly religious woman who had attended services on a regular basis. "Why this change of heart all of a sudden?" he asked.

"You know, I pray for something, and it doesn't happen. I pray and I pray and I pray, and it still doesn't happen. How am I supposed to believe in a God who doesn't answer my prayers?" the woman said.

"Ah," the rabbi replied, "but God *did* answer your prayers. The answer was no."

The point being that God—or the universe, if you prefer—doesn't always have to say yes. It doesn't mean you stop believing in the existence of good in the world; it means that you don't get everything you want. No one does.

I can no longer pick up my phone and call my dad and say, "Hi, Dad. How are you doing today?" But I can and often do remember the conversations we had when he was alive; nothing can take that from me, and thinking of him always makes me smile.

The Georgia Centenarians

In 1993, the TV series *20/20* did a show that revolved around men and women who have lived past the age of 100. Six of the participants in the show were part of the Georgia Centenarian Study, the largest study of its kind ever conducted.

One of the women showcased on the program was 102-year-old Mary Sims Elliott. The day before her interview, Elliott's 77-year-old daughter died. When the show's producer learned of her loss, he called her and suggested they schedule another time for the interview. She refused. "I want to do it now," she said, "as a memorial to my daughter."

During her interview, Elliott described many cherished memories of her daughter—of the fun they had together over the years, of the love they shared. Yes, she was grieving, but she had also had 77 years with this child. "I remember when she was 2," she said to her interviewer, "and she would lie down for her nap. She would say 'Now I go to sleep with God.' Well, sir, yesterday she went to sleep with God forever."

Just imagine how many people you would have to say goodbye to if you lived 100 years. Yet one of the things centenarians seemed to have in common was a strong sense of optimism. Rather than focusing on the hardships of their pasts—the majority of those in the study had been poor all their lives—they instinctively remembered the good times. They had a sense of appreciation and gratitude for their lives and for the family and friends with whom they shared them.

According to the researchers, the factors that contributed to the centenarians' longevity didn't include genetics or a particular diet. The subjects certainly didn't go to health clubs to work out, and none of them were financially well off. Most had to focus on what little they had and as a consequence were joyful and appreciative of what they had. Of the 96 people in the study, 86 percent were women, and more than half of them were African American. If you think about what subset of the population had a hard life in the past century, the intersection of those two groups had it pretty tough. Yet having incredibly positive views of their lives and dealing with life's hardships in the ways that they did was so much more constructive than running to a shrink or embracing the victim label. The four most common traits among the Georgia centenarians were:

- **Optimism.** They spoke often of the tendency to believe, or at least hope, that things would turn out well.
- **A sense of purpose.** Even at the age of 100 or older, they got out of bed in the morning. They knew they had something they were going to do that day that meant something to them.

- **Multiple activities.** They weren't invested in just one thing. They had their church or synagogue; they had their family and community. Volunteerism was rampant. They did all sorts of things, from working with kids to being docents in museums and working in libraries. Each one cared deeply about more than one activity, and they engaged in them all on a regular basis.

- **Flexibility in the face of loss.** This was their term for human resilience. When life hits you hard and knocks you down, can you bounce back? Some people don't. Some people lie there a long time, sometimes for the rest of their lives. Other people, like these 100-year-olds, get up and move on.

There Is No Right Way

The loss of a loved one changes the way we look at the world and the way we live in it. When a loved one dies, we change as a result of that loss. No two people cope in the same way, nor is there a right or easy way to mourn. We all experience certain feelings associated with the death of a loved one, even if not in the same progression or for the same period of time.

Loss of a Spouse

I can't tell you how many women have sat in my office longing to rewrite history. Marion, a recent widow, tearfully remarked, "I've lost my husband. We were partners our whole lives. I want him back. How can I live without him?" She sobbed uncontrollably, and I knew they must have had a wonderful life together. I knew too that she was facing a fear of the unknown. The world—the future—is a vast place when you must suddenly—and most often at a more advanced age—traverse it alone. You don't even know where your first step is going to fall. Marion was lonely, and she was afraid. I think she also wanted to know how to come to terms with such grief, how to get over it.

I asked her to tell me about her husband, and as she described him, her tears stopped. I noticed a change in her whole demeanor, her whole countenance, because then, even in her moment of despair, she was practicing a positive emotion. She simply shifted back to a time that was more joyful, more meaningful, and more full of *good*, if you will.

When she finished, I asked, "How many times a day do you do that?"

She looked at me strangely. "Do what?"

"Recall the good times."

"Not often."

"And yet you were smiling as you were telling me about your husband."

"I was?"

"You were," I said. "So what would happen if you tried more often to remember him and celebrate the fact that you had him in your life for as long as you did? That you had all these wonderful memories as a result of your time together?" Then I asked, "If you had a crystal ball, if before you were married you could have foreseen the pain and grief that is now accompanying his death, would you still have married him?"

"Without question."

"Then there must be more positive here for you than there is negative," I told her. "So why not keep your focus on the positive things? They're already in your heart. They're yours right there for the taking, anytime you want."

Psychologist Jack Bauer, PhD, of Northern Arizona University, asked a group of men and women who had lost a spouse at midlife to comment 6 months later on that person. Then he recorded and tallied up the positive and negative things each subject reported about the relationship. The results showed that those who made five positive remarks for each negative one were functioning the best 2 years later. Those who had only negative things to say—characterized by despair, anger, and bitterness—and surprisingly, those with only positive assessments were not adjusting as well.

Loss of a Child

Losing a child, even one you've never held, is unimaginable. It's nature's plan in reverse. To the woman who has miscarried, the baby she lost was as real as any other child. The heartbroken mother of a stillborn baby still grieves deeply because when the baby died, all the hopes, wishes, and dreams for that child died, too. We have all heard the stories: A premature baby, her little face obscured by wires and tubes, is unable to hang on to life. An 8-month-old boy dies suddenly in the crib for no evident reason. A 5-year-old is lost to accident or disease. Even the loss of Mary Elliot's 77-year-old daughter took its toll, showing us that there is no point at which losing a child gets any easier.

A number of years ago, on Thursday nights, Canyon Ranch had a campfire for guests at the Life Enhancement Center. When it got dark, we would sit around the fire as our ancestors had, enjoying its warmth and the pleasures of community. Watching the flames is mesmerizing; there's just something about it that lulls people into a trance-like state. On one special evening, under a full moon, the group seemed particularly congenial, and probably much like their ancestors, people began sharing their life stories.

One woman, named Evie, announced that she wanted to share something. "My daughter was killed in an automobile accident nearly 20 years ago," she told us. Then she went on, laying before us the events of that awful evening. She spoke of the slick roads and how the police came to her house that night to tell her and how she was still devastated by the loss. I suspected that story had not changed in the nearly 20 years since the accident. When she was finished, I looked right at her and said quietly, "I understand how you feel."

"You can *never* understand how I feel," she barked back. "You think just because you're a psychologist, you can understand what this feels like?"

"I'm not speaking as a psychologist," I said. "I'm speaking as a parent like you, who has also lost a child." She looked at me, stunned. "Evie," I said in a hushed voice. "Please tell us all what your daughter's life stood for."

Everyone around the fire was silent, and we all waited while she thought about it. When she finally spoke, she told us about the funeral and how so many friends, old and young, came and how people she didn't know came up to her afterward and said that her daughter had touched them in so many ways she could never know. "My daughter changed people's lives," she said. "She played the piano at a nursing home, read to the blind on her days off. She loved music and had a wonderful singing voice."

The group around the fire applauded softly. "Have you ever put that in your story before?" I asked.

"Never," she said. "But I will now. "

If you have a child, it's only natural to think, as I did, that you would go to the end of your days with that child in your life. When that timeframe is disrupted, it shakes up your world. But there are ways to transcend the grief—by turning the long or short time that child spent on Earth into a meaningful legacy. Three of the remarkable women we interviewed for this book—Linda Richman, Anne Ryder, and Joanne Cacciatore—have lost children. Each, after a time, moved forward, fueled by strengthening the legacy of that child.

- Linda Richman leaned upon her incredible sense of humor to personally cope with the loss of her son at 29 in an automobile accident. She obviously didn't make jokes about her son's death; instead she laughed about the twists and turns her life had taken. Through her humor, her universe became more manageable. Richman tells the story of going to visit her son's grave one year. She went to put a stone on it, a Jewish custom that is supposed to let the spirit of the deceased know that someone was there. But she looked around and was unable to find a stone. Then she realized that in her purse she had a small semiprecious stone someone had given her. She left this stone on the grave and went away believing, as she always has, that the universe will ultimately provide if only you look around.

- Joanne Cacciatore has touched innumerable people with her MISS Foundation for mothers in need of sympathy and support, an organization she started after the stillbirth of her daughter Cheyenne. The organization now has 71 international chapters. In addition, she successfully lobbied for the right of every parent in the state of Arizona to receive a birth certificate for a child carried to term but not born alive.

- Anne Ryder came close to having it all. She had a successful husband, a good marriage, a healthy child, and a wonderful job as a TV anchor in Indianapolis. After the loss of her son, she decided there was more to life than being on television. And harking back to her experience when she interviewed Mother Teresa, she decided to trust the universe and take a step out into the world, not knowing where it would lead. She now spends her life doing good work with others.

Life's Slings and Arrows

Loss strikes us in other areas as well. Feelings of bereavement can accompany situations such as a marriage gone wrong; the loss of your health or the health of someone you care about; layoffs; the loss of a pet; or merely unmet hopes, dreams, or desires.

Who's Going to Love Me Now?

The suffering associated with divorce is immeasurable. You grieve for the loss of the hopes and dreams you had as a couple, the image of yourself as part of a loving couple, and the support you had raising children with a partner. Then there's the toll divorce takes on your self-esteem and confidence. Many women also grieve the loss of friendships and financial security. It's not easy under the best of circumstances.

Within that loss, however, there lies opportunity. You just have to find it. I tell women they now have a chance to develop better relationships with themselves. It's not uncommon for women to be so intently focused on trying to fix the relationships-gone-wrong with their husbands that they haven't had time to think of themselves.

One of the things I've noticed about women who have a terrible time in divorce is that while they can be very competent in many ways, there is often a little girl inside who wants to be taken care of. And why wouldn't there be? It's a comforting thought, the idea that there's someone to watch over you. But it's unrealistic. You really do need to take care of yourself. If you let that little girl take over, you're going to be miserable because you're going to appear needy. And—I've said this before, but it bears repeating—one of the things I know for sure is that certain men can smell neediness the way sharks smell blood. The "Mr. Wrongs" will begin circling before you realize what's happening.

That's not to say that divorce isn't terrible. It is. My friend's daughter Jaime had been married for 22 years when her husband informed her on the Fourth of July that he was declaring his independence from the marriage. It came as a surprise, and she felt as if an 800-pound gorilla had knocked her down.

The real question for Jaime—as it is for anyone going through this kind of rift—was how long she wanted to stay down. At first, she grieved for the loss of the marriage and dreaded the embarrassing, awkward situations she knew she would face being a single woman again. She had to tell her children that a radical shift was coming—they would no longer live under one roof together as their friends' families did. She blamed herself for putting the children in that situation, believing that had she been different, perhaps she could have held the marriage together. For months, her moods swung from deep sadness to anger and then to humiliation.

Then one day, it was over. She decided it was time to move on and asked herself what she needed for the healing to begin and to reconstruct her life so that it had meaning. Instead of badmouthing her husband as the man who had done her wrong (which would have gotten her nowhere), she began to look at her resources. She had a great family, friends, and a career. Those things didn't go away. She learned to reach out to those resources and collected the support and nurturance she needed. I'm not saying the answer is to suck it up. Rather, see through the fog of the pain and look for a path to a good life.

Talk about dreams going up in smoke. Kylie Paxman, an executive at the La Costa Resort and Spa in Carlsbad, California, never even made it to the altar. Six weeks before her scheduled wedding, a stranger armed with e-mail evidence informed Paxman that her husband-to-be was cheating on her. (The "other woman," it turned out, was the stranger's girlfriend.) With all the wedding arrangements made and paid for, and 180 guests from around the country holding airplane tickets to the wedding in a small Vermont town, she had a decision to make. Because she was responsible for the cost of the weekend anyway, she decided to turn the whole awful mess into something positive, something that would simultaneously jump-start her own healing process.

She informed the guests that the wedding was off and instead invited 125 women—only some of whom had been invited to the wedding—to enjoy the scheduled dinner and reception. In return, she asked them to donate money to two charities she had chosen, the Vermont Children's

Aid Society and CARE USA. Paxman not only empowered herself but decided to use the situation to make the world a better place for others as well.

First, You Cry

The loss of good health is way up there on the list of things people grieve for. "You never appreciate your good health until you don't have it anymore," my mother used to tell me frequently. Unfortunately, that old saw has been around so long for a reason—it rings true for all of us. Elizabeth Boham, MD, who practices integrative and functional medicine at the UltraWellness Center in Lenox, Massachusetts, wrote an essay after being treated for breast cancer, entitled "I Learned More about Health from My Experience with Cancer Than from All My Years in Medical School." This excerpt speaks to her transformation in ways to which I could never do justice.

> On September 2, 1999, I was a healthy woman with everything ahead of me. On September 3, 1999, I had surgery to remove the breast cancer. For all the changes made that day, I cried. I cried for the scar on my breast and the scar under my left arm that pulled when I moved. I cried for the fear that I would not be able to have children.
>
> Prior to getting cancer, I was very driven and not always very happy. I had a need to please others and to get approval for the choices I made. I always needed reassurance, and I often did not believe the reassurance I did receive. I was hard on myself, and this led to stress, fatigue, and sadness. I thought I had achieved a healthy state through daily exercise and a good diet, but I was neglecting my emotional well-being.

When I was diagnosed at age 30, it took time for me to accept that this could happen to me, that I was fallible. In an instant, I learned that life was not about perfection and control; it was about love and being loved. Being thinner, smarter, or financially more successful lost its urgency for me as I learned how to be satisfied with myself. Looking at myself in the mirror, bald and pale after chemotherapy, I finally saw my own beauty for the first time.

It is regrettable that I couldn't love myself before, but I am grateful for the wisdom that getting cancer brings me. I can dismiss the unimportant and be decisive. I can take the time I need without guilt, time to calm down, relieve stress, and take care of myself. This illness helps put everything into perspective, and that makes life more joyful.

Two months after chemotherapy and radiation treatments, I became pregnant with my first child, my miracle baby. Ama is now 6; my second child, a son, Tismark, is 4 years old. My family provides me with immense joy every day, and the adversity I faced with breast cancer helps me see that with the utmost clarity. It taught me how to respect the needs of my patients and how to be a better healer. I now take the time to feel the joy of everyday life. I would not have believed it on the day of my diagnosis, but breast cancer has been a blessing.

A Pack of Two

If you've never had a pet, it may be hard to understand a friend's grief over the death of her arthritic 15-year-old cat or her hyperactive dog whose sprints after the mailman finally ended in vehicular tragedy. The truth is, animals have emotional lives, and for people who bond with animals, the loss of their pets is both deep and significant. Many people bond more strongly with their pets than they do with other people in their lives, and when those pets are taken from them, their feelings of grief can be as profound as with the loss of a close family member.

The summer I was working on this book, I was in Kalamazoo, Michigan, where I met a businesswoman who was building a home in the country. One day, a golden retriever wandered into the house (none of the doors had been hung), had a bit of a "conversation" with the owner, and then wandered off. The owner came back the next day, and there was the dog. It became apparent to her that the dog had been abandoned in the countryside, and they became fast friends. She took him home and kept him for a few years. When the dog died, she buried him down by the horse stable, and every time she went down to her horses, she passed the dog's grave.

When I talked to her, she said she was devastated by the loss of the animal but wasn't ready to get another dog. She said she didn't want to put herself in the position of grieving again, as she had for this beloved animal. I told her that there was another animal that needed a home: a dog or cat out there that would greatly benefit from her loving touch. Sharing that would be good for her as well.

Don't ever expect another animal to replace your beloved pet, but understand that one of the reasons that pet meant so much to you was that you knew you were a very positive force for good in its life. It was the exercise of that positive force that added meaning to your life.

There are many reasons for bereavement that I haven't listed, both personal and professional. But there's an equal number of ways to transcend the grief that attends these losses, and I'd rather direct our attention there.

Grieving in a Healthy Way

How do you go about grieving in a healthy way? Perhaps the centenarians mentioned earlier knew better than the rest of us. Most of those people were optimistic. I'm not talking about seeing-the-glass-as-half-full optimism but rather a way of looking at life that recognizes it as a series of events. Some we label as pleasurable or good, and others we tag as painful or bad, with a whole lot in between. But you needn't reach the age of 100 to start garnering some of life's most valuable insights.

I mentioned earlier that the bereaved I counsel often ask, "Why me?" or "Why did this happen to me?" and of course, there is no answer. But I always suggest that they reformulate those types of questions into ones that challenge them to take initiative and personal responsibility, such as "What am I to learn from this experience?" "How do I go about finding resilience?" and "What legacy could I begin to live out for the person I've loved and lost?" These questions place the responsibility clearly and directly on *your* shoulders. They challenge you to step into the driver's seat of your own destiny.

Happy women know that taking responsibility for your own happiness leads to growth and enlightenment, both of which are steps on the ladder toward transcending grief.

Although grief can and most likely will visit you many times over the course of your life, the pain that accompanies it doesn't need to be a lifetime companion. If you confront your grief and work at healing, your pain will lessen. I still grieve for my son, but I can talk about him today without tearing up. Do I long for him? Of course. Do I think about whom he might have married and whether I would have had grandchildren? Sure. But I don't dwell on it.

Healthy grieving allows us to go to a different place, to see things from a different perspective. As you just saw, Linda Richmond has always used humor to assuage her grief. Some people, like Mary Elliott, use their spiritual beliefs. Some of us focus on appreciating what we still have on this Earth. My awareness of my surviving children is now greater and keener than it would have been had I not lost a child. This is one of the legacies Ryan has left with me. It is an awareness that came with circumstances I didn't choose, but I wasn't asked. It happened. And what I get out of it is a consciousness that a lot of parents don't have because, lucky for them, they've never had to deal with such sorrow.

Enhancing Happiness

The following are some suggestions based on scientific studies that lead the way to freedom, hope, and healing. If you are among the bereaved, if you feel isolated in your own grief, you may want to select one or more things from the list and invest a few heartbeats in that activity.

The Gratitude Journal

Psychologist Sonja Lyubomirsky, PhD, at the University of California, Riverside, suggests keeping a daily diary in which you write down things for which you are thankful. Although she uses the term *gratitude*, I'm more inclined to use *appreciation*. To me, gratitude involves a feeling of obligation, which is fine, but appreciation is much simpler and every bit as powerful.

I consider appreciation the highest order of love because there are no strings attached. When you walk in to look at the ceiling of the Sistine Chapel, you stand in awe, as others do watching the sun set on the Santa Catalina Mountains. Appreciation is the highest emotional experience. It is sufficient unto itself, and it's what I suggest you go looking for—everyday things in your lives that you can appreciate, from the first snowfall in

Vermont to the first smile from your newborn baby, from the gentle breeze you feel through the window after a vigorous yoga practice to the delight on a child's face as she learns to ride a two-wheeler.

Dr. Lyubomirsky proved that by taking the time to conscientiously count their blessings once a week for a period of 6 weeks, the subjects in her study significantly increased their overall satisfaction with life, whereas a control group that did not keep journals had no such gain. At the University of California, Davis, psychologist Robert Emmons, PhD, found that engaging in gratitude exercises—that is, directly expressing gratitude to someone to whom you are grateful—elevated mood, raised energy levels, and for those who had certain ailments, helped to relieve pain and fatigue.

Random Acts of Kindness

In a separate study, Dr. Lyubomirsky asked her subjects to perform acts of kindness, such as volunteering at a nursing home, helping a child with homework, or assisting an elderly neighbor. Doing five random acts of kindness a week gave her subjects a measurable boost of happiness.

The late Christopher and Dana Reeve had been married for 3 years when he was thrown from a horse and paralyzed from the neck down. What helped sustain her and get her through those tough days was a formula that the couple used all the time. In an interview in *Parade* magazine in July 2004, Dana described it this way. "When you least feel like it, do something for someone else. You forget about your own situation. It gives you a purpose, as opposed to being sorrowful and lonely. It makes me feel better when things are too hard for me."

Why does carrying out altruistic acts or exercising gratitude elevate mood? First, as you saw in Chapter 4, it simply feels good to do good. Second, it puts you in contact with others, another mood booster. Volunteering distracts you from yourself and puts meaning into your life. When you matter to others, you have a sense of purpose and feel more connected, which are important ways to help anyone who is bereft.

Joanne Cacciatore found this out when she walked into a shoe store and overheard the parents of six small children trying to decide which two needed shoes the most, because that was all the money they had to spend that day. With the image of her late daughter Cheyenne in her mind, Cacciatore stepped up and anonymously handed the cashier money to cover shoes for all the children. She then left the store. The feeling she got from her gesture was the seed that grew into the MISS Foundation's Kindness Project, which gives bereaved parents a way to share their children (or other loved ones) with those who never had the honor of meeting them. The idea is to perform random acts of kindness, usually anonymously, leaving behind a little card so the person who benefits from the kindness knows that someone's life and death continue to matter.

Faith and Belief in a Power Larger Than Yourself

The science behind the power of belief is irrefutable. Study upon study shows that those who believe in a higher power have better health, better relationships, and fewer problems with stress, alcohol, and drugs. It doesn't matter if you're an atheist or a strong advocate of any religion, if you want to get on with your life after a traumatic loss, it's incredibly helpful to believe in something. It could be something connected to the spiritual realm, but it could just as easily be a mission. It could be love, it could be Habitat for Humanity, or it could be humane animal shelters. It could be reading to someone who has lost their sight or teaching a young child how to read. The possibilities are endless. The object is to get out of your own head and your own situation and experience something of greater significance. Then watch something good happen. Because you're taking action, the world is a better place.

At one level, it's a kind of basic arithmetic. Loss means something is taken away. When you have a sense of purpose, something is added, so what you're doing is reconstituting your life. It's never going to be the same life you had, but the fact is, if you really think about it, that is true from day to day. We are all different today than we were yesterday. If your sense of purpose is sufficiently strong, it not only negates the lessening of energy that comes from a loss but also reenergizes you. You can journey from being overwhelmed and trapped in the darkness to seeing the light: seeing the possibilities, seeing a mission, having a sense of how to begin a mission and restart your life.

Create Meaning in Your Life

I cannot conclude this chapter without paying tribute to a man who really shone a light on the path to transcending grief. Victor Frankl, MD, PhD, a psychiatrist who wrote one of the most important books of the 20th century, *Man's Search for Meaning*, was interned during World War II in Auschwitz, where his pregnant wife and his parents were murdered by the Nazis. During the interminable and horrifying days spent in the notorious death camp, Dr. Frankl had the presence of mind to walk to the edge of the electrified barbed wire fence and look through it to observe the beauty of a single wildflower. He was able to look around in what had to be hell on Earth and still find something of beauty. Part of what kept him going was the images he had of one day going out and talking to people about his experiences, of showing them how to not only survive but also to thrive beyond adversity.

There are still many holocaust survivors who have kept for life that paranoia that there might one day be another death camp or another Nazi around the next corner. But as Dr. Frankl explains so magnificently, if you live in that kind of fear, you will never have the capacity to see the beauty around you. And so, with a nod to the philosophy of this great man, I ask this question whenever I counsel the bereaved: "Do you choose to look at what is painful and difficult and sad in this world? Or do you look for the flower?"

Happy women know that no one gets to be
happy all the time.

There's no getting around it. If you love, you will lose. But that doesn't mean being sentenced to a life of unhappiness. Be patient, take the time you need, and allow the grief to help you discover new independence and a fresh outlook on things.

There is tremendous wisdom that is accumulated after loss. Healing takes place when we can turn our pain into something meaningful. Helping others is the key to helping ourselves. Take time to do things that will bring renewed meaning to your life. And don't expect a life without some sadness associated with memories. The trick is to learn to love or trust again—and soon.

CHAPTER NINE

Happiness and Health

*If you have health, you probably will be happy,
and if you have health and happiness, you have all the
wealth you need, even if it is not all you want.*

Elbert Hubbard

These days, you don't have to look far to know that healthy habits such as diet and exercise are essential for good health and physical well-being, but there is now growing evidence that mental health and emotional well-being are equally important—if not more so.

Are healthy women happier? *Are* happy women healthier?

Let's look in depth at how each affects the other and see what you can do to get the maximum from both—that is, what adjustments you might make to assure the best quality and quantity from the life you have.

Happiness Defined

Emotional experiences are by their very nature subjective, and that includes feelings of happiness. There will always be that element of the "eye of the beholder"—that is, different circumstances will make different people happy. It may not be all that long, however, before scientists will be able to measure the neurology and biochemistry of positive emotion just as they currently quantify emotional disorders. For now, though, "happiness" will have to remain the rather generic label we put on a whole host of positive emotions: joy, appreciation, gratitude, optimism, satisfaction, and love.

Throughout this book, we've defined happiness in a multitude of ways. You've seen, for example, that:

* Happiness is a way of being.
* Happiness comes from having a sense of belonging and a sense of purpose.
* Happiness comes from the opportunity to engage in things for which you have a passion. (Mahatma Gandhi apparently worked 7 days a week for many years. Someone asked him why he never took a vacation, and his reply was, "Why should I? I'm on vacation every day.")
* Happiness is the positive side effect of living a fulfilled and meaningful life.

If you stop to consider how differently you and I might characterize what it means to *live a meaningful life,* you can understand why happiness is so hard to define. And, having read about it for the past 150 pages or so, I'm sure you've at least started to define it for yourself.

No matter. We can both work on our definitions until the cows come home. Without our health, we have nothing.

Health Defined

Years ago, when I was a professor at the University of Nebraska medical school, I taught my students that health was the absence of disease. While many people still characterize it that way, I now consider that definition akin to saying that the absence of panic means peace of mind or the absence of conflict means harmony.

I no longer believe the absence of something defines the presence of something else. A far more pragmatic definition of health is one I discovered in a book written in 1928 by Jesse Williams, MD. Dr. Williams calls it "the optimal condition of being that allows for the ultimate engagement of life."

There are several key words in this phrase, starting with *optimal*. It connotes superlative—the most favorable or best condition. If you visualize a bell-shaped curve, optimal is right on top. Put too *little* effort into life, and you'll never get to the top of that curve. Put too *much* effort into life, and the cost of the effort is going to outweigh the rewards. People in the first category have what I call Rip Van Winkle syndrome—they sleep their way through life. People in the second category have Alice syndrome, where they find themselves running as fast as they can just to stay in place.

The next important phrase is *the ultimate engagement of life*. This involves living meaningfully and with a sense of purpose. I can think of two men who perfectly exemplify this definition of good health. Both lived with incurable conditions but lived meaningfully and to the fullest nevertheless. Both contributed to the advancement of our society in their own unique ways.

David Rabine, MD, a surgeon, was in his midthirties when he was stricken with ALS, or Lou Gehrig's disease. As time went on, he could no longer stand beside an operating table to perform surgery. ALS doesn't affect cognitive capacity, so he became a cell biology researcher. As the disease slowly robbed him of his manual dexterity, he wrote his scientific papers with a keyboard and stylus, and when the ALS progressed to the point where he could no longer use them, he had a special sensor built. By flexing his eyebrow, he could move a pointer down his computer screen to select individual letters from the alphabet and painstakingly construct words, sentences, and articles. He wrote many important scientific papers in just this manner.

Christopher Reeve was felled by an accident that left him a quadriplegic with severely limited mobility. He devoted much of his energy to staying in the best physical condition he could under the circumstances. But he also managed to direct films and work tirelessly on his foundation, which seeks ways to cure or counter devastating spinal injuries, and he still had time for his family. I'll bet if you had had the chance to ask either of these men if they considered themselves healthy, they would have said yes. The presence of physical limitations doesn't mean the absence of health.

The point is, it doesn't matter if you're overweight or underweight, if you're exhausted or well rested. You don't have to go out and run a marathon or be an Olympic skater to be healthy. You just need to engage life from an optimal place, wherever that place might be for you.

Kudos to you if decide you want to become more physically fit or eat more nutritionally sound meals—that's great. In the meantime, though, you are what you are, and that's what you have to work with. The important thing is that you have your health. What will you do with it today?

Making the Mind/Body Connection

Yes, Virginia, there really is a biological component associated with happiness. It can be found in the neural circuits that connect the brain and the body's nervous, circulatory, endocrine, and immune systems. Although the brain acts as the conductor, it is our emotions and thoughts that make the music. Emotions and thoughts that cause us to fall in love (even when we know it's hopeless) with the one puppy in the shop that's not for sale. Emotions and thoughts that activate the pathways that ultimately influence blood pressure, heart rate, immune function, and more.

Our emotions come from the limbic brain, an area in the midbrain.

You'll recall that there are three parts of the brain: the earliest reptilian, or primitive brain, which senses and reacts but does not feel; the midbrain—or emotional brain—which also houses the amygdala, which is also known as the limbic system; and the neocortex, or thinking brain, which was formed most recently and is the seat of intellect.

While the neocortex separates humans from other forms of life on Earth, it is the limbic system—that is, the emotional brain—that we're concerned with when we talk about the link between mind and body, happiness and health.

Stress provides us with a perfect example of how the mind and body interact. Subject a person to a measurable amount of stress, and that stress can show up in the form of a headache, a rash, insomnia, or hypertension. If the stress is unrelenting or chronic, the physical ramifications eventually may lead to much worse things, such as a heart attack or a chronic and painful condition like fibromyalgia.

Let's look at how this works.

A human being has two nervous systems, the central nervous system and the autonomic nervous system. The central nervous system allows us to electively pick up our cell phones to call a friend, to stop in for a double latte at a coffee shop, to lace up our sneakers before a run in the park. On the other hand, the autonomic nervous system governs physiological systems that keep our bodies up and running. Even if we wanted to, we couldn't exert much in the way of conscious control over them. The actions of the autonomic nervous system regulate respiration, heart rate, blood pressure, hormone release, digestion, body temperature, and immune function.

The autonomic nervous system, which is the one we'll focus on, is made up of two subcomponents, the sympathetic nervous system (SNS) and the parasympathetic nervous system (PNS). The SNS gears us up to perform, while the PNS calms us down.

When we're geared up, which our ancestors had to be if they were to outrun a predator, our heart rates increase (to bring more oxygen to muscles so we can run faster), our muscles constrict (to provide more strength to fight), our arteries narrow (so that if injured, we lose less blood), and the hormone cortisol is released into our bloodstreams. Cortisol makes blood sticky and more apt to coagulate, so if we're hurt, we're less likely to bleed to death.

Years ago, these were potentially lifesaving defense mechanisms, and for all our brains know, we're *still* living in that eat-or-be-eaten world. Thus, even today, while it's not likely we'll go *mano a mano* with an oversize predator, there are still times—such as when standing across the tennis court from a fierce opponent, getting this book on the editor's desk before the deadline, or auditioning for the Demi Moore role in *Ghost: The Musical*—when it is absolutely necessary to be ready to roll.

Whereas our ancestors either ate lunch or *were* lunch—the outcome being decided in a matter of minutes—many of today's situations produce stress of the chronic variety. It's that protracted stress that can take a terrible toll on our bodies.

Stay with me here. Biology class is almost over.

Here's how it happens. You've just seen that the heart beats more rapidly under stress—both good stress (such as when the man of your dreams gazes into your eyes and says, "I love you.") and bad (such as when Donald Trump announces, "You're fired!"). Those are both short-term stressors.

When the stress is prolonged, however, due to, say, an oversize credit card debt or an unhappy domestic situation, your heart works harder to keep the blood pumping through stress-narrowed arteries, causing pressure to build up within the artery walls. It's similar to a garden hose being connected at one end to a spigot with the tap turned on full force and the nozzle at the far end of the hose barely open. The result is hypertension, or more commonly, high blood pressure.

Your body has no problem with the occasional burst of cortisol triggered by a high-stress moment in the boss's office, but when those bursts start running together, a steady stream of cortisol begins to inhibit the immune system. When this continues for any length of time, it stops the body's sentries from protecting us, leaving us more susceptible to respiratory distress and diseases.

If all of this biology is getting you down, be of good cheer. These physical problems are quite fixable. All you have to do is follow the advice of Judy Garland and "forget your troubles, come on, get happy." In other words, all you have to do is find a way to add a little positive emotion to your day.

Come On, Get Happy

Positive emotions keep the sympathetic and parasympathetic nervous systems in balance. This means that if you want to compose a beautiful life, *you need be in a positive emotional state for as much or more time than you are in a negative state.*

Studies bear this out. A University of Maryland study published in March 2005 showed that laughter may actually promote physical changes in our blood vessels. Twenty nonsmoking healthy men and women watched clips from two movies that induced two very different emotional states. They saw the violent opening scenes of *Saving Private Ryan* as well as several of the funniest scenes from the hilarious comedy *Kingpin*.

The subjects' blood vessels were measured before and after seeing the movies. It turned out that overall, watching *Saving Private Ryan* resulted in constricted blood vessels and *reduced* blood flow by 35 percent, while watching and laughing at the comedy film *increased* flow by 22 percent. Laughter may indeed be the best medicine.

In a study at the University of Texas Medical Branch at Galveston, researchers assessed signs of depression, or negative affect, and emotional well-being, or positive affect. During the study, more than 4,000 subjects were evaluated for positive or negative affect based on whether they agreed or disagreed with statements such as "I feel hopeful about the future" and "I enjoy life" or "I can not shake off the blues" and "I have crying spells." The study participants who agreed with the positive statements showed decreased risk of stroke over the 6 years of the study.

Still another study, done at the University of Pittsburgh, indicated that women who are depressed and angry are more likely to have arteriosclerosis (hardening of the arteries) and more likely to make lifestyle choices that lead to this condition. The risk factors for arteriosclerosis included smoking, poor physical fitness, and lower levels of good cholesterol combined with higher levels of bad cholesterol. This study found that the participants who showed the greatest number of depressive symptoms were 2½ times more likely to practice the behaviors that increase the risk of arteriosclerosis and heart disease.

Happiness and the Immune System

There is accumulating evidence that stress, and certainly emotional responses indicative of stress, influence the immune response. We are also learning that happiness can strengthen the immune system.

A team of researchers led by psychologist Sheldon Cohen, PhD, at Carnegie Mellon University in Pittsburgh enlisted 300 initially healthy volunteers to study the effects of positive emotion on the common cold. First, each person was interviewed to gauge his or her emotional state. Next, the researchers squirted rhinovirus, the germ that causes the common cold, into each subject's nose. The participants were then questioned daily for 5 days about any developing symptoms.

The people scoring in the bottom third for positive emotions were three times more likely to catch colds than those scoring in the top third. In other words, happy people are three times less likely to get colds than unhappy people. How's that for the power of positive thinking? The study also determined that positive thinkers who did develop symptoms complained about them less. Happier volunteers were found to have lower blood levels of stress-related hormones such as cortisol, which influences high blood pressure and also affects the immune system.

Hormones and Happiness

Hormones are one of the very important classes of chemicals active in your brain, and hence they affect how women perceive themselves and the world around them. Women's brain circuitry and hormones are much more attuned than men's to the emotions of others. At the tender age of 3, girls already are better than boys at making eye contact with other people and gathering information from their facial expressions. By 10 or so, as their brains are flooded with estrogen, girls are well on their way to re-creating the behavior patterns of their mothers. According to *The Female Brain*, by Louann Brizendine, MD, girls are more likely than boys to take turns, forge connections, and create community. During menopause, she says, estrogen levels drop, and personalities can change as women find expressing their independence more pleasurable than nurturing. After age 50, women initiate 65 percent of the divorces in the United States.

Women's hormones can have a tremendous impact on their happiness, according to Molly Roberts, MD, MS, a family physician at Canyon Ranch, and the behavior patterns they trigger should be acknowledged. Validating these feelings, she says, will make life easier for everyone involved.

What's So Positive about Positive Emotions?

You have just seen how positive emotions affect our physical health, but the benefits don't stop there. Positive emotions greatly impact our mental and emotional well-being as well.

- Positive emotions, even the fleeting ones such as joy, hope, optimism, love, contentment, and gratitude, help us to grow as people, energize us for positive action and problem-solving, improve the quality of our relationships, and have an overall cumulative effect on emotional well-being.
- People who habitually experience positive emotions become more resilient over time.
- People who keep a positive attitude through an ordinary day's bumps and hiccups may have a greater ability to cope with adverse circumstances and bounce back quickly from them.
- In bereavement, people with a positive emotional bent adjust to their loss relatively quickly and move on sooner to setting new life goals.
- People who generally experience life with a positive mindset have better relationships and work cooperatively with others.
- People who have a positive outlook generally report a better quality of spiritual life. They have greater peace of mind and certainly tolerate and recover more quickly from the inevitable problems life presents to each of us over time.

How can you go about building a more positive life? Well, unlike with the responses of your autonomic nervous system, you do have control over your behavior, and you can nurture positive emotions through attitude (which includes optimism), by building connections (i.e., active involvement with community, family, and friends), and by creating meaning through some type of spirituality (such as religion, meditation, yoga, and so on).

Happy women know that a good attitude,
valued relationships, and a meaningful life are
the central ingredients for happiness.

MOLLY ROBERTS, MD, MS

It is important to remember that menopause is not a disease. It is a time of transition, one that has the potential to be the best time in a woman's life. Menopause is a biochemical occurrence in our bodies and brains, and it produces changes on a daily basis. But menopause is also a time when your body no longer allows you to be dishonest with yourself.

At the start of menopause, most women believe their estrogen is diminishing to nothing, but actually it's all over the map; older women experience raging hormones much like adolescents do. And it's those raging hormones that are perhaps responsible for the changes in their emotions.

When hormones are shifting is actually a great time to take notice of things that are going on in your life. Those are the times that keep you *emotionally honest*.

Often, if a woman falls into a bad mood, or she has the blues, or she's just not happy, she excuses her behavior by citing the biochemical response to what her body is going through. If she's a grouch, it's PMS or "that time of the month." If she's fighting all the time with her daughter or her mother, or if she hates her job, it's menopause kicking in.

Well, maybe yes, but maybe no. What may actually be happening is that her hormones are coming to the surface more at those times, and they are bringing with them the "real" feelings she has and making it harder for her to push those feelings under the rug. If she is upset over random annoyances, okay, we'll blame it on the hormones. If her upset has a theme, her biochemistry may be giving her an opportunity to look more deeply at what is in and out of balance in her life.

Optimism

Here's a question for you: With whom would you rather have lunch—Chicken Little, who is sure to interrupt you and the waitstaff with urgent warnings about the sky falling, or the Little Engine That Could, with the limited but unquestionably sunny four-word vocabulary: *I think I can!* No

This is a perfect time to look at what is happening around you and to make the shifts and changes that will make your life better. For example, you may find yourself unusually argumentative with your spouse at these times. If you examine those arguments, the results will have the potential to make your relationship stronger. Conflict is bad only if it isn't resolved. Not talking about your feelings doesn't make them go away and may even accentuate them.

Not many people realize that both women and men have estrogen and testosterone floating around in their bodies. Menopausal women have proportionally more testosterone as they age, which may make them want to go out and take on the world. Men during this time have proportionally more estrogen and may be more into nesting. As things begin to change, if both partners can shift together, it makes for a very happy state of affairs.

The happiest menopausal women in my practice are those who are willing to look long and hard at what is happening within them physically and emotionally and are really taking stock of their lives. Many are thrilled with the renewed freedom that comes with the empty nest and with the opportunity to refocus their attention on themselves. When women come to see me during this time, I have them identify what brings them joy and what brings them sadness or anger. Then we try to figure out how to maximize their time with joyful activities and minimize those that don't feed them physically, emotionally, and spiritually. Who knew that moodiness could play such a key role in a woman's happiness?

contest, right? This, in a nutshell, is the most basic example of optimist versus pessimist.

Optimism is a disposition some people seem to be born with, while others can't seem to win for losing. The good news, however, is that optimism can be learned.

There are many reasons to come at the world from an optimistic viewpoint, the most important of which could be that it's good for your health. Research suggests that optimists live longer, happier, and more satisfying lives.

Lionel Tiger, PhD, is a sociologist from Rutgers University whose book *Optimism: The Biology of Hope* tells us that it was biologically adaptive for our ancestors to develop a sense of optimism. Dr. Tiger explains that humans tend to give up on tasks associated with negative consequences. Without optimism, he says, a guy might have sat around the cave all day waiting for the rain to stop. Now we all know if he had sat around the cave, he wouldn't have been out there hunting, and it's obvious that wouldn't have been a good thing. What sent him out, spear in hand, into the cold and rain? The same thing that sends men in raingear and umbrellas out onto the golf course in spite of ominous weather reports.

Studies show that optimistic pregnant women have lower risks of postpartum depression. Other optimistic women exhibit lower mortality rates from heart disease and cancer, recover from surgery faster, and have healthier immune systems. Not bad for starters—and the list goes on.

The Optimistic Tipping Point

If you find yourself walking a fine line between optimism and pessimism, here are some tools to help you move closer to the optimistic tipping point.

- **Switch thoughts.** As soon as pessimistic thoughts come into your head, quickly replace them with positive ones. Remember Serena from Chapter 1? She learned to crowd out her painful memories by appreciating the beauty around her and basking in the love of her family.

- **Switch gears.** When problems arise, rather than bemoaning them, consider the possibilities and then set out to solve the problems. This is what Julie (Chapter 2) did by employing the principle of Kaizen, which allowed her to eventually play the piano in front of just about anyone.

- **Switch friends.** Avoid people who drain your energy by judging you, belittling you, or just overloading you with their problems. With friends like that . . . well, you know. Lauren (Chapter 6) was faced with just such a situation while married to David. Life turned beautiful the day she walked out the door for the last time.

- **Walk the walk.** In other words, act as if things are just great, and it will fast become a self-fulfilling prophecy. Optimistic people move faster, talk faster, and project an upbeat attitude. When someone asks how you are, say you're "terrific!"—even if you've just gotten your third speeding ticket. You don't need to advertise the downside, especially to anyone who relishes hearing about your bad luck. You know who I mean!

Of course, there is a place in this world for pessimists, and to withhold their due would be unfair. In fact, some people are actually *paid* to be pessimists. School crossing guards, for example, are on high alert for anyone who might come careening through a stop sign when children are crossing the street. Physicians need to look for signs of disease in our bodies if they are to properly make a diagnosis. Some people are just plain pessimistic, though. I think they are more beset by fear that things will not work out and would rather expect the worst and be surprised than hope for the best and be disappointed.

There are many bright young researchers coming along to lend their intelligence, creativity, and innovation to the question of what constitutes the good life. One of these outstanding scientists, Susan David, PhD, is a young woman who came to the United States from South Africa by way of

Australia, where she completed her doctorate. What she has to say on the topic of health and positive emotions is below.

"Only Connect"

Those two words are the directive for forging bonds suggested in the epigraph of E. M. Forster's novel *Howard's End*. Forster was on to something, even back then, as his characters struggled with the dilemmas of making connections in a Victorian period that preceded World War I.

SUSAN DAVID, PHD

A growing area of positive psychology research suggests that positive emotions are absolutely central to people's experience of well-being. And yet, one message that I would hate to give people is that positive emotions are *all* that matter. Negative emotions—fear, anger, and sadness—exist, too, and that's just a fact of life. So if people start to feel sad, and because it is an unpleasant feeling they try to sweep it under the carpet, the repercussions can be counterproductive.

If happiness is the goal, it's essential to be open to all of the messages that emotions provide, whether those emotions are positive or negative. Of course, it's best to try to create positive emotional experiences in your life. The more you focus on things that are going wrong, the more those things become central to your perspective.

Psychologists see this a lot in relationships. A couple who might be experiencing some difficulty will go off to breakfast and discuss the problem, and they'll go out to lunch and discuss the problem, and then they'll go to dinner and discuss the problem. The intention is a good one—to actually solve the problem. But when couples give all their attention to what's wrong in their relationship, the things that are really good get minimized or ignored. That's why people can go to couples therapy for years and years and never get any closer to actually solving the problem. The problem has taken on a life of its own.

Because evolutionary biology made it practical 80,000 years ago for humans to run in packs (safety in numbers and all that), our limbic systems drive us to seek out emotional connection. Thanks to that drive, you put out and receive thousands of messages in a single passing wave to a friend you might see on the way into a movie. The speed with which you pass and your facial expressions tell her if you're interested or not in hearing about her trip to Tahiti. Give a quick raise of the eyebrow to the stranger seated at the other end of the bar. If he nods back in your direction, your limbic brain will go into overdrive calculating what that tilt of his chin

After acknowledging the message that your emotions are giving you, you need to move on from recognizing how you're feeling to asking, "What am I going to do about it?"

Let's take for example a woman who is incredibly depressed and is spending 20 hours a day sleeping. She may be thinking, *My life is awful. My friends hate me. I've got no family. I'm broke. All I want to do is sleep.*

Let's say I see that woman in consultation, and after listening to her, I say, "It sounds like your life is dreadful; let's talk about your dreadful life." We'd go nowhere! Instead, the question I would ask is, "What is *different* about today? Today you made it to the therapy session. You got dressed, you had a shower, and you came to my office. What did you do differently today that got you here?"

What I'd be trying to do is get her to focus on what is already working despite her circumstances and how she can do more of it. If I can get her to identify the fact that having an appointment, having some kind of structure, having something to go to makes a difference for her, then that's something we can actively build into her day. If I do that again and again, soon I start crowding out the negative parts of her day with positive matters and have her heading in the right direction.

meant and extrapolating it into future relationship scenarios—particularly if you're single and he looks like George Clooney.

Women are hardwired to seek deep connections and lasting friendships. It's the women rather than the men who generally hold an extended family together. A women's circle of close friends is almost always larger than her husband's, and she is guaranteed to spend more time nurturing those friendships.

The strength of those connections is reflected in our health as well. A study of more than 4,000 people showed a direct link between the size of their social circles and the length of their days. The larger the circle, the longer the life. Even a woman's coronary arteries tell you something about her friends. That's right. The more friends, the clearer the arteries. But before you put down this book to go round up a whole bevy of new friends, hear this: Quality counts, too.

Earlier, I described how happy my grandparents were despite having little in the way of money to spend on luxuries. What they had, it seems, was an extended family that lived nearby and with whom they spent time, plus a bunch of good friends who were mostly neighbors. It was all about relationships.

This holds true as well for the Georgia centenarians in Chapter 8. You may remember that more than 80 percent of the original 96 people enlisted were women, and about half of those were African-American women. Despite being part of one of the more oppressed subsets of the population in this country in the past 100 years, they were happy women. So what did they know? They knew that they had each other.

Connecting is not only about relationships, however. It is also very much about human touch—and about love. Chris Crowley and Henry Lodge, MD, tell the following story in their excellent book *Younger Next Year for Women*. A group of rabbits were kept in individual cages stacked up to the ceiling in a research laboratory. They were being administered some type of cholesterol so that the researchers could study the effects of plaque buildup in their arteries. After a while, it was time to examine the rabbits, and it turned out that those in the lower tiers had 60 percent less plaque in their arteries than those in the upper tiers.

The finding stymied the scientists for a while, until they spent some time observing the laboratory attendant. She loved animals and patted and fussed over the rabbits she could reach. Being of short stature meant she could reach only those on the lower levels. When the rabbits' positions in their cages were switched, those that had at first been left alone also did well. The patting and touching did more than smooth their soft fur.

Not long ago, I was talking to one of the guests at the ranch about the merits of volunteering and how it can really bring perspective to your life. She agreed and offered this story, which she witnessed firsthand as a volunteer in the pediatric ward of an inner-city hospital. One day, she said, an elderly woman walked into the emergency room of a Newark, New Jersey, hospital. She was carrying a blanket-wrapped baby, who looked from a distance to be quite small. It turned out that the "baby," named Melanie, was 22 months old, and when the woman, a neighbor, had remarked earlier to the mother that there might be something seriously wrong with Melanie, the mother literally handed the baby over to the older woman and said, "Here. Maybe you can fix her."

The first thing the ER staff did was weigh Melanie. She weighed 12 pounds, could not stand, and had never crawled. They later learned she had not been deprived of food so much as of love. No one ever held little Melanie for very long. Her mother claimed that with five other kids, she simply "didn't have enough time."

When Melanie was admitted to the pediatric ward, her diagnosis was "failure to thrive." The pediatrician assigned to her case left a single prescription: Melanie was to be held as often as possible, around the clock, by any nurse or volunteer who had a free arm. Within 3 months, she was standing and weighed in at 20 pounds. Eleven months later, on her last day at the hospital and just shy of her third birthday, the smiling child, now far too heavy to carry around for very long, ran down the hall with a fistful of balloons to bid goodbye to the nurses on the pediatric floor. According to them, there wasn't a dry eye in the place as they stood watching "their" little girl smile and wave and grab tightly to the hand of her future adoptive mother.

Such is the power of touch.

Daniel Goleman, PhD, a psychologist and the author of *Emotional Intelligence,* wrote in his *New York Times* column of a friend—a college professor much loved by his students—who has been battling cancer against all odds "through a grinding mix of chemotherapy, radiation, and all the other necessary indignities" for more than 10 years. Dr. Goleman believes that one of the things that has kept his friend around so long is the fact that through it all, he has had a steady flow of visitors who genuinely care about him. Love can make us resilient.

This is not news. For quite some time, research has linked good health, speedy recoveries, and longer life with social connections. What *is* news—or was several years ago—is the discovery of what are known as mirror neurons. These are brain cells that mirror the emotions of the people we are with. Because we replicate in our own brains precisely what others are sensing and feeling in theirs, emotional closeness allows the *biology* of one person to affect that of another. This may explain why when two people who care about one another are together, they are so often of a single mind. It's why when you're feeling great, and your son comes home from school to announce he didn't make the team, your mood vanishes with his words. It's also why it is so important to visit loved ones during times of illness, even if, as Dr. Goleman says, you don't know what to say.

Sexuality

Sexuality is one of many factors that indicate the level of well-being. It's also one of the most complex aspects of humanity because it connotes so many different meanings, depending on the person in question. I recall a scene from an old Woody Allen film where a man is sitting in a psychiatrist's office, expressing his disappointment by saying, "It's a shame, Doctor; we hardly ever have sex anymore. Maybe three times a week." Then the scene changes, and the wife is sitting in the doctor's office complaining that they "have sex all the time, maybe three times per week."

If you take the idea of sexuality to a higher level, it can connote anything that gives pleasure. For example, those who enjoy painting could be said, at least from one perspective, to be sexually expressing themselves. Anyone who has ever had the pleasure of viewing a great masterpiece, listening to an exquisite symphony performance, or feeling a fresh mountain breeze caressing their skin understands that to experience pleasure means to find the essence of life's energy.

Sexual pleasure is one of the great physical joys of life, no question. Beyond its role in creating a family, today's woman views sexuality as a means of expressing who she is and what she needs to make her happy. For many, however, this produces a problem. Romance and sexual fulfillment are so prevalent as themes in books, films, songs, and theater that there is no question women are socialized to believe there is a fantastically fulfilling world out there. If they're not part of it, they often either feel they are the only ones left out or worse, spend an extraordinary amount of time chasing after an elusive rainbow.

I asked Evelyn Resh, MPH, CNM, a sex therapist at Canyon Ranch, about how and where sexuality fits into a happy life. Her response follows on page 194.

EVELYN RESH, MPH, CNM

Our society is based on productivity: We need to be able to measure things to feel life is working for us. It works that way with sex, too: We tend to determine how good our sex lives are by how many times a week or month or year we "do it" or by how many orgasms we have.

Commonly, when I see a patient, I'll ask her, "Are you sexually satisfied? Do you feel as if your needs are being met?" And she'll tell me how many times a week she has sex. Then I'll say, "That's not my question. My question is, 'When you are sexually intimate, do you feel emotionally satisfied? Does it bring you pleasure?' "

If someone is sexually intimate three times a year, and it's deeply moving to her, then to me, she is sexually satisfied. If someone is sexually active four times a week and dreads every moment, then she is not a sexually satisfied person. And yet, it's that measurement in and of itself that the person relies on as a statement of sexual success.

Sexual pleasure cannot be measured. How do you measure your pleasure in a massage? How do you measure your pleasure in orgasmic response? How do you measure your pleasure in listening to your favorite opera? You can't. It just is. It's the same with eating. Rather than encouraging people to enjoy and appreciate what they're eating, we measure how good the food is by how much they eat.

Sexual energy can't be measured either. It's different for each of us, and it is not specifically about the sex act. Rather, it is involved in everything we do and is totally integrated into our being.

There are high and low ends of the sexual energy spectrum, and women fall all along the continuum. Women may find themselves at any point, depending on their temperament and the environment they grew up in. Infants come into the world with different temperaments. You can see it in the hospital nursery the day they are born. Some cry all the time, some are placid, and some keep moving and looking around. In much the same way, some girls come into the world with an enormous amount of sexual energy, and others are more forebrain focused, more analytical. To have a satisfying sexual life, it's essential to recognize that there's a temperament difference—and it usually lasts a lifetime.

Those at the low end of the range, women who have little feeling for sexuality, can still be happy and sexual, as long as they recognize where they are on the spectrum. They need to proceed at their own pace and

do best if they find a partner who more closely matches their temperament, so there isn't sexual appetite dissonance. That actually can be
said for women all along the spectrum.

Women who have low sexual energy often come from homes where the
parents are more intellectually inclined. I learn about them by asking certain questions. For example, I might ask them to tell me something about
what their family meals were like, and they will say, "They were three
squares. We always had dinner at 6:15. My mom wasn't a great cook."

If I ask if they had a pet, they say, "No, no. No pets."

If I say, "Can you tell me something about your room when you were
growing up?" they answer, "I don't really remember it that clearly."

When asked about their favorite color, they say, "Umm, well, I kind of
like blue."

In contrast, my conversation with a woman who is on the opposite
side of the continuum might sound like this.

"Okay, so tell me something about your family meals."

"My family always had lunch on Sundays at Grandmom's. We had
everything. Everything! Lots of conversation. Kids running around.
Great food."

"Did you have animals growing up?"

"Yes, of course, of course we always had at least one family dog, usually two. We had a cat; bird feeders."

"Tell me something about your room."

"Oh, my God, I loved my room! I had posters of John Lennon all over
the place."

"What's your favorite color?"

"You know, it's hard for me to decide, I really, frankly love green as
much as I love blue. I can't really tell you what one is a favorite."

These people are sensually alert and engaged and grew up in envi-
ronments where their limbic brains were constantly being activated.

Can those at the low end of the sexual energy scale be elevated, or
at least be brought to neutral? In some cases, yes—if they are interested
and willing to work on it. But in other cases, even if they want to change,
they can't. The important thing is that women can be happy with their
sexuality at either end of the spectrum, as long as they are aware of and
understand their sexual temperament and its relationship to their sen-
sual engagement and energy.

Spirituality

A growing number of research studies tell us that people who have spiritual beliefs are on the whole happier and healthier than those who do not. "Believers" have lower blood pressure, lower risk of stroke, healthier hormone levels, better immune system and heart function, and better relationships. They also have fewer problems with alcohol and drugs and mental illness.

When I say spirituality, I'm not referring specifically to organized religion or traditional religious beliefs. Having a spiritual life simply means believing in something beyond yourself. This can include any higher power, meditation, prayer, tai chi, or just the realization that you're part of a greater picture in the universe.

Religion and Happiness

Does religion bring happiness? Are religious people happier than nonreligious people? It seems so. In one study of more than 160,000 Europeans, both churchgoers and nonchurchgoers agreed to answer a few questions. Of the weekly churchgoers, 85 percent reported being very satisfied with life, while only 77 percent of the nonchurchgoers reported high satisfaction. That's a measurable difference, if only a modest one. Another study looked beyond church attendance to religious experiences, including prayer, and found a similar pattern.

There are perhaps three reasons why religion and happiness are directly related. The first has to do with social support. People who are with other people—whether they worship together or knit together—are generally happier, particularly when the other people are friends or family. The second reason concerns an understanding of what is important in life, which is closely associated with religion for many people. Finally, we must consider that religious experiences themselves—that is, closeness to God or whoever is representative of the higher power—promotes a sense of calm and well-being. I should add, however, that the chicken-and-egg dilemma applies here. No one has answered the question about which comes first— does religion make people happy, or are generally happy people more religious?

Meditation

Why are some people unhinged by the sorrows of life, while others appear to be relatively resilient?

One answer may be the practice of meditation.

Meditation has been around for more than 2,500 years. Its principal goal is to cultivate positive human qualities, to promote flourishing and resilience. It has long been known that meditation reduces stress, but with the aid of advanced brain-scanning technology, we can also say that meditation directly affects the function and structure of the brain, changing it in ways that appear to increase attention span and improve memory. Sara Lazar, PhD, a research scientist at Massachusetts General Hospital in Boston, presented early results of an investigation that showed that the gray matter of 20 men and women from the Boston area who practiced a Western style of meditation called mindfulness—that is, focusing on an image or sound or the breath—for 40 minutes a day was thicker than that of people who did not.

Whereas Dr. Lazar's interest lies in the physical changes associated with meditation, other researchers are more interested in the emotional link. Many studies suggest that meditating affects parts of the brain associated with positive thoughts. One of the most prominent studies is ongoing and directed by Richard Davidson, PhD, of the University of Wisconsin, a pioneer in mind-body medicine. Dr. Davidson has flown Buddhist monks

197

from India and Nepal to his laboratory at the university just to monitor the electrical impulses of their brains before, during, and after meditating. What he learned was that the prefrontal lobes of the monks' brains were lit up almost continuously, not only during meditation. Activity in the prefrontal lobe illustrates positive emotion, or to put it more simply, the monks were in a good mood.

Dr. Davidson likens meditation to exercise. If going to the gym and exercising can change the body, he says, exercising the mind in a particular way can produce similar changes. He considers happiness to be a skill that can be learned in much the same way as one learns to play an instrument. Practice makes you better at anything. The monks he has studied for years practice mindfulness hourly and daily, which he correlates with their overall sense of well-being. That they do it so often may be why they appear to be happier for longer periods of time than the rest of us.

A Walk in the Woods

The most accessible pathway to the true spirituality is all around us, but it is of such magnitude that we often miss it all together. It is awe-inspiring and provides moments—if not hours—of peace and serenity. It is a God-given right of every creature on this earth.

I'm speaking, of course, of nature.

If you're looking to destress, detox, or just delight yourself, you need look no further than the natural world. Take a walk through the woods at dawn and listen to the birds as they awaken; stroll on a beach at sunset and breathe in the smell of the ocean; wade through a shallow stream and feel the mud between your toes—or just sit in your backyard and watch the grass grow.

There are hundreds of ways to find your own Walden Pond. All you need to do is go looking.

Running the Happiness Marathon

As I said at the start of this chapter, the meaning of happiness will necessarily vary from one person to another since, like beauty, its definition rests in the eye of the beholder. Nevertheless, the good news is that we all can play an important role in making ourselves happier and, as a result, *healthier*. Happiness, it seems, is just a muscle that needs to be flexed. And that means employing the tools we've included throughout this book, such as interrupting negative thoughts and replacing them with positive ones, building on your strengths, setting personal goals and striving toward them in small increments, and connecting with people who give you energy rather than those who take it from you.

I won't elaborate because you've read all of them by now. But if I had to select the one tool I consider to be most important, it would be this: *Treat yourself well*. What do I mean by that? I mean indulge in a hot-fudge sundae every so often.

Go on, cheat a little. It'll do you good.

10 Qualities
of Happy Women

Over the course of nearly 30 years in practice, and in fact over my lifetime, I have come face to face with scores of women. Some of them have been virtually unscathed by life's trials and tribulations, and yet they were not as fulfilled as one might expect them to be. Others have been steam-rollered multiple times by life's losses and hard knocks and have transitioned beyond their experiences to create lives full of purpose, meaning, and fulfillment.

I began to wonder how it is that some so blessed can go unfulfilled, while others whose lives have been derailed appreciate and cherish life in spite of its persistent difficulties. Why do so many in the latter group still identify themselves as "happy women"?

I thought if I could understand what was going on with those who have found the good life despite tough times, or even those who have *always* been happy, then quite possibly that wisdom could be shared with others so they could experience greater meaning in their own lives.

My coauthors and I sought the answers from a variety of women—some of whom we knew and some, as I stated in the introduction, to whom we were led for the purposes of this book. Of the many women we interviewed, we selected 18 who we felt best represented the characteristics, behavior, and persona of a happy woman. (You'll find a short biography of each at the end of this chapter.) These women come from states all across the country and represent a veritable microcosm of society. They are old and young; rich and poor; well and not-so-well educated; single, married, and divorced.

With the transcripts of their interviews in hand, we started looking for patterns that came together in various combinations so that we might identify which qualities are most likely to distinguish a "happy woman." We came up with the 10 listed below. As you will see, most of the women we selected had more than one of these attributes and often had more than a few.

I wish we had ample space to include each woman's full story—that's how good they were—but we don't. Instead, we selected certain segments that we felt most clearly conveyed the essence of what they had to say. The words, however, are all theirs.

As you read these vignettes, you will no doubt recognize yourself or your circumstances in some or even many of them. Perhaps by seeing firsthand what these women have done, some of the choices they made and the reasons they made them, you will find the right combination of multi-dimensional living for yourself. I hope their examples will provide the courage or even just the information you need to make some essential life decisions of your own.

Here, then, are the qualities of happy women.

1. Believing in Yourself

I was getting a PhD when I started my family and decided to stay home with my three little ones. I left both my job and the PhD program in order to become M-O-M. I was actually quite surprised that I got so much flak from so many people. "You're giving up your career? *And* the Ph.D.? You're ruining your life!" But I did it anyway.

Suddenly I had a new identity. I was a housewife and a mother. When I'd go to a party with my husband and someone would ask me what I "did," I would answer politely, "I stay at home with my kids." Then they would ask my husband what *he* did. When he said he was a doctor, they couldn't turn to him fast enough. I got their backs. Like I was a nonentity.

As my kids got a little older, I decided to go to medical school, and as I bandied the idea about, I got flak once again: "*You're leaving your family! You're abandoning them!*" I struggled with the decision, wondering if I was doing harm by following my dream. My husband perfectly framed the decision to be made. "The kids are going to be a lot happier with a happy mother," he said, "so figure out what's going to make you happy and do it." I realized I wasn't going to win in some people's eyes no matter what I did. So I did what I thought would be best for all of us. I went to medical school, and the kids were just fine. They're all now very happy, well-adjusted teenagers who still like having me around, so I must have done something right.

Molly M. Roberts, MD

It was tough after the divorce. Very tough. My children didn't have the same things that other kids had. Even with child support, I had to take a hundred different jobs. One time, we ended up living with a family in their summer home. I watched their kids and in my time off, taught exercise classes on the beach. I did whatever I could to make ends meet. But through it all, I never lost sight of what *I* wanted to do. And that was to be my own person, to have my own identity and my own career. And that's exactly what I have done.

Loretta LaRoche

When dealing with a child who, according to society, is "less than perfect," you have to let go of judgments about yourself. Particularly since other people will surely look at you when your child misbehaves and say you're a bad mother or that there's something wrong with you as a parent. It's finding the strength to be able to see those judgments as *their* issue and not yours that gets you through it. Before we truly understood Kyle's autism, I blamed myself. I decided that I had done something to create what was wrong with our child. Once I could let go of that, once I could see that I am out there as a woman, as a mother, as a wife, as a friend, as a sister, as a daughter—always doing the best I can—then when other people cast judgment on something I might be doing, they're less effective. No one can create unhappiness in me if I believe that I'm doing my best.

Jenifer Westphal

Shortly after I joined *Playboy*, the decision was made to recruit a president and chief operating officer. The man who was hired didn't do as well as expected, and it was clear that there was going to have to be a change in management. So I went to the board and to my father and proposed that rather than begin a search for a successor, which would take many months—and then he or she would need time to learn about the businesses and build enough knowledge to make good decisions—that I be named president.

And they agreed. And that is how, at the ripe old age of 29, I was named president and COO of Playboy Enterprises.

People love this story, but I point out that it's only a terrific story because it has a happy ending—we're doing just great. I also hasten to add that the reason this all happened is because I had the *chutzpah* to step up and propose myself for the job. And the only reason *that* happened was because I didn't know enough to know what I didn't know.

Christie Hefner

My parents were both Holocaust survivors who suffered terrible family losses in the camps—they each lost almost everyone before they met each other. Afterward, they always shared everything—even when they had nothing. My father came from a very successful business in Poland, and everything was taken away from him. After the war, once again, he rose and became successful. What both parents taught me was this: When you believe in something, no matter what is taken away from you, if you have life, you can accomplish it again. And often not only the same thing, but even better.

Helena Striker

The success of my company was not the measure of me—it happened through the work of so many other people. I don't think I really found out who *I* was until about 5 years ago. I think I just found my voice. It was around the time Simmons College awarded me an honorary undergraduate degree, and I felt I had finally arrived. I don't know quite what did it, what it was, but it was a mixture of love and acceptance, of their belief in me and perhaps of other things too that finally allowed me to think, *perhaps I have something the world wants to hear.*

Lois Silverman

2. Knowing Your True North

You can't just have someone say, "Look, I know you haven't been happy for 40 years of your life, so why don't you just get up today and say, 'I'm going to be happy?'" It won't work. You have to think about yourself and isolate what it is that you really like about yourself, what makes you *feel* happy. Is it listening to classical music or jazz or soft rock? Is it watching a TV program, crying at a movie, or buying a pair of shoes? Is it being with a friend? There are a million things. But you have to realize that it doesn't work if you're looking outside of yourself for somebody else to make you feel better. You have to do the things that make you feel good, by yourself and for yourself.

Helena Striker

We lost our son before he ever even took a breath of life, but still I received from him the greatest gift. What my son gave me was the appreciation to know that life is incredibly precious. Instead of living for "maybe someday soon," I realized that I must do now all the things that I really want to do. And what I knew in my heart was that I was really tired of anchoring the *Evening News*. I wanted to be home with my daughter. I didn't want to spend another moment missing her softball games or her recitals—missing these very precious times.

Anne Ryder

There is no question that there is a consciousness to my happiness. The thing that brings me to it is being in nature and trying to find a sense of proportion in everything that's there. The silence lets you hear yourself think. You can't lie to yourself. You are open to all of your feelings. But you need a quiet place to make these things happen. Nature is what does it for me. Other than love, it's the most restorative thing on this Earth.

Judy Seinfeld

What I love about where I am today is knowing that I'm not perfect. You bet I've made mistakes, but at least I now know who I am and where I'm going. And I feel like I no longer have to explain anything to anyone.

Carrie Kennedy

I come from a working-class, blue-collar family. Both of my parents worked their whole lives in factories. We worked because we had to, not because we had careers. I've worked since I was 14. What drove me was wanting to get out of that environment. Working hard was my way out.

After college, I went to work in the White House during the Ford Administration, became press secretary to a senator, and ended up with my dream job, producing television shows for ABC News. It was a frenetic existence—I was always on the road with no life of my own—but it was an incredibly exciting life. A real dream come true.

I was in my thrities before I started realizing that something was missing. I never did the things that most people got to do, like go out on dates, spend time with friends, live like a normal person. And it was soon after that that I ran into a very dear friend—a big-time agent in New York. I told her about all the exciting things I was doing, and she said, "Susan, be smart. Don't make the same mistake I did."

I asked what she meant.

"I bypassed the good things in life because I thought my work was more interesting than any man could ever be."

Not long after that, I met a man who seemed just perfect for me, but we both knew the relationship wasn't going to work if I was off traveling for work all the time. And my girlfriend's words began to resonate with me. I was looking at 37 years old, and I was afraid I was going to miss having a life.

So I mustered up all my courage, and I quit. Just walked away. For the first time since I was 14, I wasn't working.

It all went very quickly after that. We got married, I got pregnant, and we moved into a little house with a white picket fence in the suburbs of Washington, DC. I remember waking up the first morning and walking to the window. I heard the birds singing. I saw mothers pushing strollers, and I thought, "Oh, my God, what did I do?"

And then my son was born. I was so in love with this baby that I started doing something that was really quite remarkable for me. I started living in the moment. Not someone else's moment, not a future moment, not a past moment. Most important, not a *past* moment. It wasn't about, "Wasn't I a fabulous producer? Didn't I live this fabulous life?" That didn't matter anymore. And I vowed not to look at my New York City girlfriends and care that they were climbing the ladder and becoming the vice presidents and presidents of this, that, and the other thing. This was my time. I was being a mother and going to playgroups. It was glorious.

I began to love the suburbs. I made great friends and was very busy with the children (I had another baby by then). Then I met someone from *Vanity Fair* magazine who asked me to do a freelance project for her, and when I finished it, she asked me to do another. So I started working again, part-time, at home. It was a gift. I could raise my kids and also do something else, something that challenged me in a different way. I worked when it was convenient. And if I was on a conference call with someone important, and my babies were making a lot of noise playing underneath my desk, I would happily tell the caller, "I'm working at home." And here's the news. Nobody cared!

If I needed to, I worked at the playground. Someone took a picture of me sitting in one of those playground tree houses with a 35-page fax—in those days, it was all rolled up—careening down the slide, my kids playing happily below.

I'm not saying that's the way everybody should live, but it worked for me. It gave me a way to occupy my mind, make some extra money, and not be crazy. I didn't care that I wasn't vice president or executive producer. It just didn't matter to me.

Maybe I didn't have it all, but I had enough.

I laugh sometimes when I see the young, aggressive, ambitious kids, and I think, *Yeah, that used to be me.* And that was great. And it's great still for some women who feel the need for it. I have a very fulfilling life. I suppose I could do more, bite off a bigger chunk of my career, move up. But I really don't want to. My kids are still young, and they still need me. And that is my priority.

Susan Mercandetti

3. Taking Personal Responsibility

I grew up in the sixties, a highly charged political time in societal history for African Americans. The sixties were the time of busing and desegregation in the schools. We were under constant scrutiny. And there was always the threat that you would never, no matter how hard you tried, be good enough. At the time, one of the things my parents stressed was: You must get all A's. You must be better than everybody else—you can't be perceived as "not as good." Perform higher, better, faster. Be as perfect as you can. There was never, ever, a downtime. It was exhausting.

I'm 44 now. Today my generation is the benefactor of affirmative action. What that means is that when I go somewhere, I still can't always be myself. At certain times, I have to be representative of my whole race and my whole gender. For example, when I was working at the bank, I got the sense that if I messed up, then no other African-American woman would be hired behind me. And that totally reinforced the must-be-perfect thing.

Yvette Hyater-Adams

We are limited only by how much we limit ourselves. We are all capable of tremendous love and compassion—we are capable of achieving anything we want to achieve. But when we start saying things like, *Oh, I can't do this . . . I don't have the time to do that . . . I don't have the energy to do this . . . I don't have the intellect to do that . . .* , that's what limits the expansiveness of the human potential.

Joanne Cacciatore

It was the first time in my life that I told myself: *You know what? You made a choice. Everything else in your life has been about your choices, and now it's time to make good ones. I mean, what else could go wrong? Twice divorced, no kids, poor family life—what else could possibly go wrong? Nothing.* That was actually the most freeing moment in my life, when I realized that nothing else could go wrong. That was the time to begin to rebuild—the time for the phoenix to rise.

Lynn Brewer

How do you forgive yourself for spending so much of your life on something that isn't working? Coming from a perfectionist father, one of the most difficult things I had to learn was that it's okay to admit mistakes. And sometimes saying them out loud is more healing and beneficial than anything. I remember the first time I sat down with my son, when he was about 7 or 8 years old, and said, "I'm very sorry. I've really made a mistake. I should not have done this." I can't remember what it was exactly that prompted me, but it must have been something pretty big. I also remember thinking that I would have given anything for my father to have done this with me.

Carrie Kennedy

I have a strong belief in social justice and have the view that it is an obligation of all of us to work toward making society a more fair and just place. I believe in kindness and good manners toward all.

Christie Hefner

I watched a rerun of the Olympics last week. I think the fact that an athlete even makes it to the Olympics is great. But whether he or she comes in first or not, to me that's just a number in a record book. I give them a great deal of credit, make no mistake, but there comes a point in time when we're all forgotten. And as far as I'm concerned, it's what we do and how we make the most of things while we're here that in the end is the important part.

Ruthie Cohen

My father, as he lay dying, said to me, "Take care of the rest of the family." That's a terrible burden to put on a 15-year-old, but it also gave me a sense that he believed I could do it. And what gave me the confidence to try was believing, as I still do, that there's no such thing as "can't." You can if you try. I also believe there's no such word as *let*. No one can let you do something. You choose to do it, or you don't choose to do it.

Lois Silverman

4. Having Courage

Divorce was huge for me, particularly since I was raised in a Catholic family. But my husband was an alcoholic, and I remember finally thinking to myself, *I would rather be alone and lonely than not be the person that I can or want to be.* So I told myself, *Okay, you opened the door. You either run through it, or you shut it again. But if you shut it again, you're going to continue this life. What's your choice?* So I went through the door.

I knew it wasn't going to be easy, and it wasn't.

Carrie Kennedy

What I noticed in the bank where I worked was that many of the women executives were gradually taking on the behavior of the men. But I felt one of the reasons we were in those ranks was to modify them, not to become *like* them. So I had to really step back and think about who I was and what it was that I wanted. And that put me on the journey of going to my boss, who was the CEO of the bank, and saying, "You know what? I don't want to do this anymore."

He said, "What? You can't quit. We just repositioned you!"

And I said, "Yes, yes, I can. Watch me."

Yvette Hyater-Adams

From a very young age, I was a competitive ice skater. My coach ultimately became the US Olympic coach, so striving for perfection and not quitting was deeply ingrained in who I was. I was on the ice at 6:00 in the morning, skated for a couple of hours, went to school for 4 or 5 hours, then went back to the ice arena. I could never please her. This was back in the days when you did school figures on the ice and they judged you on how close you came to perfection. I was very good at it, but my coach would say, "This looks like hell—you're wobbling all over the place!" Being constantly subjected to such negative comments was unbelievable. I was 8 years old!

But I couldn't stop. My father was a professional baseball player, and if I would come home and say I wanted to quit, he would say, "You can't quit today. You have to give it at least 6 more months."

As I grew older, I left skating behind, but not my search for perfection, because my father ingrained in me that you continue to strive to make things right, even knowing you may never get there. I tried to live his message in so many areas of my life, but perfection is never within anyone's grasp. It's almost impossible to achieve it.

After two failed marriages, I decided it was time to leave St. Louis. I was recruited to work at Enron in Houston. This was the absolute dream job for me. I headed a risk-management group. Every deal that Enron did went through my department. We analyzed the deals and then looked at where the risks were. My specific responsibilities were to brief senior management and the board of directors about the off-the-balance-sheet partnerships of the chief financial officer.

Within 6 months, though, I began noticing some activity among the officers that looked very much to me like bank fraud. Soon the company began manipulating the prices of power, and I saw the resulting California blackouts. I also witnessed the chief operating officer overstate Enron's financial position to both the media and stock analysts. I tried talking about what I had seen to people inside the company, but each person I went to told me I was mistaken or to just stay out of it and not say anything.

It was a terrible time. I was torn because the money and the security kept me tied to the company. It was like being tied to a horrible marriage and staying because you have the house, or you have the kids. Eventually, though, I decided that the money was just not worth it. The stress was killing me—I truly believed it was—and so I decided to go outside the company to Enron's employee assistance program. But even *they* turned me away. The woman I spoke to said, "Ma'am, inasmuch as our fees are paid by Enron, I can't take your call. You'll have to hire a private lawyer."

That's when I went to the media and then to the head of the Energy and Commerce Committee. It was almost as though everything that I had done to that point in my life was preparation for that moment.

It took me a year to get over it. Then one day, I remember thinking: *Wouldn't it be nice if at the end of the year I could look back and say that everything that I've done this year has been* good? That was when I took the money I had left and started The Integrity Institute. That has been an absolute blessing for me because for the first time in my life, it's not about me. It's about making the world a better place. I make less money today than I've ever made in my life, but I'm loving life. I absolutely love life.

Today I live with my husband on a farm in a town of 400 people. Most of them don't know what Enron was. I live a very obscure life. Here, I'm no one special. I'm just somebody who had an experience. The institute is *less* than a nonprofit right now, but I'm working toward something great. And I know that as a result, at the end of my life, I will be able to say I have reached what perfection now means to me. It won't matter what size my body was, it won't matter what kind of car I drove, it won't matter how much money I had in the bank. What will matter is if I have changed a small part of the world for the better.

Lynn Brewer

5. Being Altruistic

Serving others can help take your mind off yourself. Doing for others is what life is about! In serving others with that giving intention, we all can reap the benefits of the world's abundance!

Suzanne Mikols

My life is broken up into what I call two periods of time, BC and AC. The BC stands for "before Cheyenne," and the AC stands for "after Cheyenne." My AC life began in 1994. At the time, I had three young children, ages 6, 5, and 3. Cheyenne was my fourth daughter, who died during childbirth. There was no medical explanation for her death. She went all the way to her due date. Her room was already prepared; the car seat was waiting in the car. And she died 10 minutes before she was born.

It was such a dichotomous experience to give birth and death at the same time. There aren't words that can describe what it's like. You've got the physiological changes, the hormones, the milk, the changing of the body, everything that tells you life goes on, concomitant with the emotional loss.

I was in such an adversarial relationship with my body; I felt like my body killed her. All I would have had to do was hang on for 10 more minutes, and she would have been fine, but instead, my body took her life. Because I blamed myself for her death, I began a downward spiral into a very dark and abysmal place. I lost a great deal of weight; I found it difficult to care for my children. And I found myself alone, feeling very isolated from the rest of the world.

To hide, I would sit on my closet floor, not wanting to wake the children, with my knees drawn up to my chest, crying and rocking back and forth and back and forth. This went on for weeks. It was the only place I found comfort.

And then one day, for no particular reason, I decided it was time to do something, so I took the phone book into the closet with me and started calling support groups for grieving mothers. I got five disconnected phone numbers. There were no working groups! I couldn't imagine that in a society where death is so much a part of life, that we had no compassionate way to deal with this. Right then and there, I said to myself, *Someday I'm going to change this. I don't know when, I don't know how. But someday, I'm going to help someone like me who can't find her way off the closet floor.*

A short while later, the state sent me a copy of Cheyenne's *death* certificate but no birth certificate. So I called them and said, "I have my daughter's death certificate, but you didn't send me her birth certificate." When I told the woman on the telephone the circumstances of my daughter's death, she said, "You didn't have a baby."

I didn't have a baby? I had 12 stitches from the episiotomy, breasts overflowing with milk, hormones bouncing all over the place, and as a reminder, a baby's room that was complete down to the little stuffed animals in an empty crib. So I said, *What do you mean I didn't have a baby?*"

And she said, "Ma'am? You had a fetus, and the fetus died. Until it breathes, it's just a fetus."

I started shaking as if I had to shake some contamination off me. I couldn't bear that someone just told me my daughter Cheyenne didn't count.

A few weeks later, I started doing research, and what I found was that babies who died the way that Chey died weren't counted in infant mortality data in the United States. None of them were given birth certificates because only their deaths were recorded, not their births. Which makes absolutely no sense. *How can you die if you never were?*

And yet there was a state law mandating final disposition—so they are essentially saying that you have to bury or cremate somebody that never was. Right then and there, I promised myself that someday, when I had the emotional energy, I would change that situation, too.

In 1999, I started researching how to pass a law in the state of Arizona, and I found the way. I got a sponsor for the bill and lobbied for a year. And in the end, male and female, Democrat, Republican, every single person with whom I met supported this bill, and in 2000, the bill was passed in the legislature with unanimous support. Arizona was the first state in the United States to initiate what we call the Missing Angels Bill, requiring and mandating the issuance of certificates of birth for stillborn babies.

Cheyenne was the first stillborn baby in the United States to receive a birth certificate. I didn't expect it. I didn't even consider that they would support the idea of retroactivity. I did it because I didn't want women to experience what I experienced. What I was fighting for was to change history for all women in Arizona. To date, we have been successful in passing the bill in 16 other states since 2001.

While all this was going on, I started the MISS (Mothers in Sympathy and Support) Foundation. I started by doing home visits with women who had been through my experience, but then it graduated to a support group where people could talk to each other and meet each other and exchange phone numbers. It really took off, and the support groups just grew and grew, and before I knew it, we had 25 to 30 regular attendees at one group. Today, we have 76 support groups around the world, and our Web site gets 1.5 million hits a month. We have 27 online support groups for anyone who has lost a child at any age and from any cause. We all have different experiences, but we're all living our lives in the absence of someone that we love: our child.

If you can find a way to channel trauma in your life, if you can find a way to take the negative emotions in your life and turn them into someone else's happiness or compassion for someone else, that is a self-fulfilling act. For me, it has always been a given: Cheyenne's life resonates in everything I do—always. And it's because of that, that I believe in my heart that one day I'll see her again.

Joanne Cacciatore

6. Embracing Optimism

My fundamental optimism is a character trait, but it was certainly nurtured and enhanced by the attitudes that both of my parents had. I grew up living with my mother; she has a really wonderful outlook on life and a very kind attitude toward people, both of which I think influenced me. And one of the most charming qualities of my father is that in spite of his tremendous financial and previous success, he has never lost his delight in life or his sense of joy and wonder.

Christie Hefner

I often wondered what kept me there. I mean, there were plenty of days when my situation was chewing me up alive. But I had the children to consider. Some days I told myself, *I may not have his love, but he's a wonderful provider, extremely well-liked and even revered in our community.* And he was fun. Sometimes.

Other days, I guess maybe I was too scared to leave. And still other days, I rationalized: *Okay, so I don't have 100 percent, but I have a really good 50 percent, and my 50 percent of a marriage is better than a lot of people's 100 percent.*

I also told myself happiness is something you choose. If you want to be unhappy, you can roll around in your unhappiness all day long. Or you can just count your blessings and go on and do the best you can. I immersed myself in my children. I was working part-time, I was a Scout leader, I managed the children's soccer teams and their swim teams. My cookie jar was always full—kids loved coming over here because even when my kids weren't here, they knew I would listen to them. We would sit and talk, and I got a lot of reward out of being a great mom.

So that was my life. I decided to be happy, damn it, and I was. And still—I admit it—I was ever hopeful.

Hope Cooper

If people could just lighten up and see life in a positive way, they would find more inner peace. When someone is more peaceful, then their family is more peaceful, their community is, and then, perhaps, the world can be as well.

Loretta LaRoche

Sadness *feels* very permanent because you can't see the other side of it, but what if tomorrow is better? If there is anything I have learned in my life, it is that in an instant, things can get better.

Lynn Brewer

I was born crippled. My feet from the knees down were clubbed. It was as if you turned your hands backward and around. Both legs looked like that. It took me a great deal of time to walk. I've been asked, "What was the prevailing feeling growing up?" And it was one of great joy and happiness. Whether it's because of how I choose to remember my childhood or that it actually was, the majority of my memories are excellent ones.

My mother refused to allow me to pity myself. No one around me did. So I had "crunkled feet." "So what?" she'd say. It was not in the greater scheme of things a big deal. My sister has bad eyes. When we were growing up, my mother said, "So you have the feet, she has the eyes. There is no 'can you top this?' in this family."

Ruthie Cohen

7. Being ProActive

I grew up in a perfectly normal sort of Ozzie and Harriet kind of family. But when I chose to marry, I picked a man who couldn't have been farther from that image. In fact, he turned out to be the architect of my darkest days.

Much as I was crazy about him, we were really not very compatible. He drank too much, and we fought all the time, and he was verbally abusive. But once I said, "I do," my commitment was to stay married no matter what. Even after we had children, things continued downhill for us. I think he wanted me to be like his mother, who always has a smile on her face, never complains, and always does what her husband says. But I couldn't be that person. As a result, he no longer had any use for me, and he left. And so, with three small children, a big mortgage, and an unpaid-for car, I found myself alone.

It turned out to be fortunate for us all around because after he was gone, I realized that the model of married behavior that I had been providing for my children was just terrible. I feared that my daughters were going to seek out partners who might abuse them or that my son could become an abusive husband. I think far beyond loyalty or sticking together for their good, children need models of adult people who are honest and calm and seek to resolve their problems. Pretending that there is no problem or allowing yourself to be mistreated is so damaging for young children.

We had no choice but to move to a much, much smaller house. And we got on with our lives. We were actually quite happy. Tired—at least I was—but happy. We didn't have much, but we had enough, and we had each other. To make ends meet, we took paying boarders into our little house. I got a job teaching science at a school, and when I could, I wrote for *Science Weekly* and *Parent and Child*. I made about $600 a month cooking lunches and selling them to the teachers at school. I did science birthday parties, I did rollerblading clinics, I did summer camp work. I just always said yes to every opportunity, and I got my kids to help me. As the kids grew, I continued to be promoted in my career, and today we're managing pretty well.

Everyone asks me how I did it. I tell them that the first thing that you have to recognize within yourself is that you're braver than you know. The second thing is, I think it's a primary responsibility of parents to cultivate optimism in their children, to show them that having faith and working hard can solve problems. I also think optimism is so important to having a happy outcome in your life.

Optimism, but also bravery. You just have to be brave the first time, and you'll realize that things are going to be all right. The biggest step for me was to admit to myself that I was terrified. But I resolved to move ahead anyway. I just kept telling myself over and over: *I'm going to be okay. I'm going to be okay.*

And I am.

Julia Berry

8. Appreciating Life

Since I lost my daughter, I realize that every single moment, every breath, every second, is a gift. Every single second. Of course, I drive my four surviving children absolutely insane because I am constantly kissing them and hugging them and saying, "Look in my eyes. I love you, I love you, I love you." And they are like, "Mom! Okay!"

Joanne Cacciatore

I don't really remember any part of the accident other than that I was driving and the other car hit mine head-on. Most of the early days of my recovery are still a blur, too. After being unconscious for weeks and strapped down in a hospital bed with a neck brace immobilizing my head, I can only remember opening my eyes for the first time and thinking how lucky I was just to be alive! I could move my fingers and toes. That was good. I had always been a singer, and from that hospital bed, I quietly tried out my voice. When I realized I could still sing, I was ecstatic! I asked for a mirror and was thrilled to see that none of my teeth were damaged.

My brain, unfortunately, was not so lucky.

The accident left me with a serious brain injury. I spent quite a while in a rehabilitation hospital, and even when I was finally able to go home, I was not right. My whole world was constantly moving. When I'd walk, I'd walk on an angle—as if I was leaning to the right side—but it felt to me as if I was walking straight.

It was a terrible time. My life had always been so fast, and here I was being made to do everything so slowly—step by step. When I got through one thing, whether it was cooking my breakfast or taking a shower, I would have to decide if I should try something else or go to sleep. I wasn't sure when I was going to be able to walk alone down a set of stairs. I couldn't even speak the way that I could before. Different things would come out of my mouth. I wasn't me anymore.

I had to learn patience, to allow myself to heal and to give myself the right to make mistakes. You have to learn how to surrender to what you cannot do. That was the hardest thing for me. Being in control was always my most important thing. As a corrections officer, you are *always* in control. And when all of your control is taken away, you are stripped of everything.

One morning, as I was facing another Mount Everest, I started to feel very sorry for myself. I thought, *I can't do this anymore. I'm too tired. I wish somebody else would just take all of this away from me.* I sat in the middle of my bedroom floor, literally ready to throw in the towel. I wanted so badly to give up. But something wouldn't let me quit. I started talking to myself. I told myself, *These thoughts aren't helping me at all. I love life. I am going to fight to live. I want to be alive, and I want to experience everything in life. I'll get through this. I'll get through this. I'll get through this.*

And right there and then, I took back my life.

For much of my life, I haven't moved forward in some things because of basic fears, like maybe I'm not a good-enough singer, or maybe I'm not a good-enough this or that. Those kinds of things stop you, and you limit yourself. What I learned from this experience is that if I could get over this mountain, there was going to be nothing I couldn't do. And that's how I feel. I mean I literally believe that I can do anything. In time, I will do anything and everything.

I'm not sure if I'm ever going to be like I was before. There are still some slight differences, but your body does have the capability. It is beyond anything that man can build, and the way it can rejuvenate and heal itself is limitless. There is one thing I can say, however, without reservation: I am not going to take anything for granted again. Not ever. The injury that I endured created a genuine appreciation for everything! Being alive is the most fantastic gift! There is such joy in taking an ordinary shower, visiting with friends, or listening to my cat's singsong purr. A sunset every evening brings great humility and gratitude.

Because my brain was injured, so much of what I do and see is new and fresh! This must be how a child experiences life as it is first introduced to an unknown experience. Sometimes I am a child again. All this from a brush with death and a brain injury. How lucky I am!

Suzanne Mikols

We all have the opportunity to tell our own stories in whatever way we choose. I could say very truthfully that I come from a poor family, and I had very few opportunities; that I started working at 14 because I had to and that I had to work hard for everything I got. I could tell that story, but the story I choose to tell is that my work ethic was the greatest gift I could possibly have gotten, because if you're not the smartest kid on the block, you'd better know how to work hard. And that's my story. It's not about what I lacked, it's about what I worked hard for, achieved, and greatly appreciate.

Susan Mercandetti

9. Being Wise and Sharing Your Wisdom

Don't envy what someone else has. Be grateful for what you have. Don't look at someone else and say, "Oh, my God, that house, that car," because you don't know what's inside there. You don't know what's going on behind those closed doors. My grandmother's favorite thing to say was something to the effect of "If you hung your dirty laundry out on a line along with everybody else's, you'd take yours back." That's the whole point. People spend a lot of time aspiring to have something or be something, and when they get there, there're never any happier than they were when they started.

Ruthie Cohen

It's amazing what you can do when you don't know that you can't do it.

Loretta LaRoche

As a woman, if you see you need help, if you see there's a place you can go to find some way to feel better about your life, then you must do it. You do what you need to do. You take the information and you use it, and work it, and make mistakes, and maybe even find yourself unhappy again, but if that happens, you just ask yourself once more: *How do I move from this unhappiness now?* Just keep going until you get what you need.

Jenifer Westphal

No matter what you're doing, make time in your life for silence. Silence, meditation, prayer, whatever you call it, make time just to listen. You don't have to fill it up with words. Even if you're having trouble concentrating, try to do it every day. Every day. And watch and see what happens as a result; see if something in your life does not change.

Anne Ryder

I find that sometimes when people are unhappy, it's because they don't have the proper perspective on their situation. Happiness can be enhanced on a number of levels, one of which is by being more knowledgeable and aware of other people's lives and the world. And one really good way to do that is through reading. That, apart from just the joy of reading and of having books transport you to other places, can help you feel less isolated and more aware of and attuned to others.

Christie Hefner

A lot of times people pray to God to give them a sign, and it always reminds me of that old story of a guy on the roof with the lifeboat. There's a storm all around and the town is flooding, and the guy climbs to the roof and says, "I need God to save me." And people in lifeboats come by one right after another, and they ask the man, "Do you need a ride?"

"No, I'm waiting for God to save me."

Another lifeboat comes by. "Do you need help?"

"No, I'm waiting for God to save me."

Eventually he drowns and gets to Heaven and asks, "God, why didn't you save me?" and God says, "I tried to. I sent you three lifeboats!"

We wait for our lifeboats, and sometimes we don't recognize them.

Anne Ryder

If we could see how harshly we judge ourselves and how much we expect of ourselves, we would see that that's not helping us accomplish what we want to. It's actually letting go of judgment, coming to yourself and saying, *I'm an awesome person who is contributing so much value to my family, to my husband, to my friends,* that takes you to a happy place where you can first start to get things done.

Jenifer Westphal

∴

Revisit the past, but don't live in it. Learn from it, and shape the present and the future from those lessons.

Loretta LaRoche

10. Persevering

My life, as I remember it, starts when I was 8 years old—when my father was run over by a truck and killed. I kept asking my mother and my aunt, who lived with us, *"Where's Daddy?"* "He went away," they told me. There was this conspiracy of silence where nobody would say anything, and I was told not to ask. And because I was a good little girl, I didn't. But I still believe that the fact that nobody answered me back then is what makes me want so much to be heard these days.

Fear became my shadow after that, and for most of my life, there was always something looming in the dark. At 19, I got married and quickly created the family of my dreams. My son was born right away and my daughter soon after. Four people around a dinner table—the perfect family. *But it didn't stay that way for long.*

When my children were still very young, two things changed. First, my husband became an inveterate gambler, and second, I had my first major panic attack. If I had to go somewhere—anywhere—I broke out in a sweat and just couldn't do it. The attacks, slow at the start, increased with such strength that ultimately I stopped leaving the house altogether.

And I never went out again for the next 11 years.

At first, I managed quite well. I had company often and lots of parties, and I managed to just stay home by bartering. For example, if I needed food, I'd watch a friend's children in my home, and she would do my shopping. The year was 1964. At that time, nobody had even heard of the word *agoraphobia*. There was actually some happiness, some joy that I got during this time. I loved my kids. I loved being a mom. I loved to read. And I loved not going out. I loved not facing the world. I was really quite content in the house. It was mostly just me and the kids because my husband was often off gambling.

I stayed that way until 1975, when my husband brought home a magazine with a small ad on one of the back pages that read "Long Island Jewish Hospital is looking for participants for a research study." I was shocked when I read it. I had every one of the symptoms that they described. So I called the number and said I'd like to participate in the study. The woman who answered said, "Great! Come to the hospital, and if you fit our parameters, we'll sign you up."

I said, "Miss? Maybe you don't understand what this is about. *I haven't been out in 11 years!*"

She said, "Sorry, Ma'am. The only way we can assess you is if you come here."

At that point, I wanted to be well so badly I was willing to try anything. My girlfriend agreed to drive me. We ended up putting a blanket over my head so that I couldn't see the outside world. That's how I walked to the car, and that's how I went into the hospital. At the hospital, I filled out all the papers, put the blanket back over my head, and went home. Three weeks later, the study leader called, told me that I had agoraphobia, and enrolled me in the study.

The treatment included behavior modification. They took us all over—to public places, to shopping malls, on trains, and for the first time in my life, I stepped onto an airplane. I flew alone to Washington, DC, and came right back. And that was it. Done. After that, I was able to go anyplace and do anything.

During this time, my husband continued to gamble. His gambling increased until slowly but surely he lost everything we had—our house, our cars, and our furniture. Everything. At that point, the children were grown, and I decided I had had enough. I threw him out and then had to give up our apartment. And there I was, at age 47, homeless and penniless. My sister started giving me $200 each week to survive. For a while, I slept on friends' couches, until finally I got a job. I went to work for a casting director and made enough money to move into my own apartment.

Several months later, after life had begun going well again, I got a knock on my door. It was the police informing me that my son had been killed in an automobile accident.

How do you live in a world after losing a child?

There is no guidebook.

You do what you must and what you can. I sat *shiva*—the Jewish period of mourning—for 2 weeks, and then I started cleaning my apartment. I was like a madwoman, cleaning every single thing in the house, taking the mattress off the frame, taking down the curtains, washing the curtains, taking fixtures down. I scrubbed until my hands bled, and then I scrubbed some more. I'm not sure why, but I know part of it was about survival. It was about breathing. It was about staying alive.

In time, I knew I had to get back to life, but now I had no idea what life would be for me. I was not only back to square one, I was back to nowhere.

I had to learn to live again.

Eventually I opened my own casting business, and almost overnight I was making more money than I had seen in my lifetime. But was I happy? Not really.

Thinking it might help to have a change of scenery, my daughter treated me to a short stay at Canyon Ranch. At the time, I couldn't imagine why, because I don't hike, I don't bike, I don't swim. I don't even *walk* if I don't have to. But my daughter had been there and had heard this man speak. He was a therapist named Dan Baker, and she thought he'd be good for me.

She was right, of course. Waiting in his office, I saw through a window a guy get out of a pickup truck and head toward the building. I was used to the New York doctors in suits and ties, and into the office walks this man from Nebraska who was dressed like he was going to jump on a horse and ride away down the trail. He sat in the chair opposite mine, and we started talking. About a half hour into questions and answers, he stopped me in midsentence and said rather ungraciously, "You're absolutely charming, Linda, but you're full of shit." Talk about love at first sight!

"How am I full of shit?" I asked him.

"You're lying to yourself. You're avoiding all the important issues in your life."

And thus began the peeling back of an onion named Linda.

After that, I returned to Canyon Ranch whenever I could. One day in his office, Dan said, "Why don't you consider speaking to the guests here at the ranch?"

"Speaking about what?" I asked.

"About your life."

"What *about* my life?"

"Well it's been a pretty crazy life," he said. "It might be helpful for others to learn from your experiences."

At my first lecture, I walked to the lectern holding all sorts of notes. Dan was in the audience that evening, and he came up to me, gently took the papers out of my hand, and said, "Talk from your heart." It was a very successful evening. And each time I returned, the audience increased, although I was never really certain why. I did make them laugh, though. I knew that much.

I started giving workshops where 10 or so people would sit in a room together, and we would discuss their personal issues. We would work on those issues in a very humorous way, and they would walk out feeling great and with their issues resolved. Often, they would thank me and tell me how I changed their lives, and I always replied, "That's wonderful. But can you please tell me what I *did*?"

The workshops became more and more popular. One day in the middle of one session, we were discussing certain meaningful experiences in our lives, and suddenly this woman started crying. When I asked her what was wrong, she said, "I was thinking about my baby who died 3 days after she was born. They never let me see her, and I never gave her a name." And she started sobbing and collapsed on the floor. Immediately I said, "Okay, everybody. Lets all get down on the floor with Nona." And we did. And we embraced her. Then I had this thought. I said, "Let's have a baby-naming ceremony." We got together a whole bunch of pink helium-filled balloons. We went outside and made a circle. I asked Nona, "What name were you going to give your baby?" and she said, "Wendy." So we all said Wendy's name together and let our balloons float up into the air. When I saw her the next day, she said, "You have changed my entire life. You gave my baby a name. You made her real for me." That's when it occurred to me that maybe, just *maybe*, I was doing something of value.

During this time, someone suggested I put my story into a book, so I figured, why not? I became a published author, and soon I was speaking about my life all over the country. I talk often about how I managed to hold onto my sanity and become a truly happy person despite everything. I've learned that being able to see the humor in things my whole life has truly been a gift. I think it's laughing with and at life that has gotten me through it. You want to be happy? Laugh. That's it, right there. You *gotta* laugh.

Linda Richman

Biographies of Interviewed Women

Julia Berry is currently director of St. Columba's Nursery School in Washington, DC, which is well known across the country for including children with special needs. She also writes for *Science Weekly* and is a former oil spill cleanup specialist who worked in Alaska during the pipeline-building years.

Lynn Brewer, a former Enron executive, is author of *Confessions of an Enron Executive: A Whistleblower's Story.* She is founding chairman and CEO of the Integrity Institute, which independently assesses and certifies corporate integrity, and is the subject of a 2007 documentary to be presented at the Nobel Peace Center in Oslo, Norway.

Joanne Cacciatore, LMSW, FT, founded the MISS (Mothers in Sympathy and Support) Foundation, an international nonprofit organization, 2 years after the death of her infant daughter, Cheyenne. In 1999, she spearheaded the Missing Angels Bill, ultimately making Arizona the first state to issue certificates of birth for infants who died during or prior to childbirth. If you ask her how many children she has, she'll reply, "I have four who walk and one who soars."

Ruthie Cohen is an artist and the founder of Banner of Hope, an organization that raises funds to provide underserved Phoenix women with education about breast health and treatment options following a diagnosis of breast cancer.

Hope Cooper is living happily with her new, 100 percent partner. She now has everything she needs: work, love, and grandchildren.

Susan David, PhD, is an internationally known authority in the field of positive emotions. A researcher at Yale University, Dr. David leads workshops and seminars that apply emotional intelligence abilities to performance effectiveness.

Christie Hefner is chairman and CEO of Playboy Enterprises. She has long been active in empowering women and has founded several women's organizations, including the Committee of 200 and the Chicago Network. In 2005 and 2006, she was named to the *Forbes* list of 100 Most Powerful Women in the World.

Yvette Hyater-Adams is founder of Renaissance Muse, a transformative language arts practice that uses creative and expressive writing to heal, empower, and transform the lives of individuals. She is also a poet, writer, and organizational development consultant.

Carrie Kennedy is corporate program manager at Canyon Ranch in Tucson.

Loretta LaRoche is an international consultant and lecturer in the field of stress management and the star of six award-winning specials on PBS that address the power of humor in overcoming stress in everyday life. Her books include *Relax—You May Only Have a Few Minutes Left* and *Life Is Not a Stress Rehearsal*.

Susan Mercandetti is a senior editor at Random House.

Suzanne Mikols holds a degree in music. For more than a decade, she has been a corrections officer at the Las Vegas Detention Center, where she is also currently a professional standards unit officer.

Evelyn Resh, MPH, CNM, has practiced medicine and midwifery for more than 20 years. She has cared for teens and women of all ages and is currently director of sexual health services and programming at Canyon Ranch.

Linda Richman is a summa cum laude graduate of the school of hard knocks. A certified grief counselor and author of *I'd Rather Laugh: How to Be Happy Even When Life Has Other Plans for You,* she currently lectures nationwide on the healing power of laughter.

Molly Roberts, MD, MS, is a physician at Canyon Ranch and codirector of the Synchronicity Center for Mind/Body/Spirit Medicine in Tucson.

Anne Ryder, a TV reporter, columnist, and speaker, has earned numerous honors for her reporting, including the prestigious Gabriel and Wilbur awards, the Edward R. Murrow Award, and 10 Emmys. She is currently president of Ryder Media.

Judith Seinfeld has passed every test life has thrown her way, including the loss of two husbands. She did it by being appreciative of what she has had, knowing that her response to any event in life is hers alone, and continually seeking to grow in wisdom.

Lois Silverman received a $300 scholarship to attend nursing school from the Jewish Orphans of Rhode Island in 1958. After working as a nurse, she went on to found CRA Managed Care (now Concentra Managed Care) and ultimately the Commonwealth Institute, an organization that, through peer mentoring, provides women entrepreneurs with the tools and resources they need to grow successful companies.

Helena Striker was born in 1949 in Poland to two Holocaust survivors. Her family was expelled in 1956, moved to Israel for 3 years, and eventually immigrated to the United States. Inspired by her parents' survival instincts, their optimism, and their ability to begin again and again with true happiness in their hearts, she has lived her life trying to make a difference to others in the world.

Jenifer Westphal runs the Kyle Westphal Foundation and Kyle's Treehouse, which are dedicated to providing parents a sense of community while they search for a treatment, intervention, or therapy for their autistic children.

What Happy Women Know

Happy women know that they can have meaningful,
fulfilling, and happy lives regardless of life's
circumstances.

....

Happy women know that good enough
is always good enough.

....

Happy women flow gracefully into the next decade
and the next because they find things to love about
themselves throughout their life cycles.

....

Happy women know that their worth is not determined
by what they have or how they look but rather by
successful relationships and emotional well-being.

....

Happy women know that admitting a problem exists
is the first step toward changing it.

Happy women understand that no matter what they own, they will always feel a bit insecure about having enough and being enough, but they don't let these feelings rule their lives.

. . . .

Happy women don't play the comparison game, because they know there will always be someone who has more than they do.

. . . .

Happy women know that possessions are never enough to deliver happiness.

. . . .

Happy women know they can be rich for life if they focus more on what they have than on what they want.

. . . .

Happy women know that if you want to take care of others, you must first—or simultaneously— take care of yourself.

. . . .

Happy women understand that today is all we can be sure of, and they know how to make the most of it.

. . . .

Happy women know that saying no to others gives you the opportunity to say yes to yourself.

. . . .

Happy women know that downtime is not a luxury; it is essential to well-being.

Happy women understand the importance of having personal power, which means their lives belong to them.

. . . .

Happy women know that taking personal responsibility for what they have and haven't done leads to a powerful and fulfilling way of life.

. . . .

Happy women know you can't control your destiny, but you *can* participate in it.

. . . .

Happy women know that forgiving doesn't let the offender off the hook; it lets *you* off the hook.

. . . .

Happy women understand the three steps to self-forgiveness:

• Acknowledge the lesson you learned.
• Recognize that you're now in a different place.
• Know that you may make a new mistake tomorrow.

. . . .

Happy women are never alone because they don't abandon themselves.

. . . .

Happy women never see a bad situation as pervasive or permanent—and they don't take it personally.

. . . .

Happy women know that courage is taking constructive action in spite of fear.

Happy women know that happiness is not the art of building a trouble-free life but rather the art of responding well when trouble strikes.

. . . .

Happy women know that before taking one more step up the career ladder, it's wise to know who and what is supporting that ladder and where that step is taking them.

. . . .

Happy women know that if you're looking for someone to share your life—including your career—you have to be proactive, and you can't compromise yourself. If you try to make your partner bigger by making yourself smaller, the relationship won't work.

. . . .

Happy women know that with each phase of life, they give up something, but they also get something in return.

. . . .

Happy women know that part of their identity is tied to what they do, but they never let what they do become their whole identity.

. . . .

Happy women know that you can have it all, just not all at the same time.

. . . .

Happy women know that grief in itself is not a trap. Believing that you can never transcend it is.

Happy women know that taking responsibility
for your own happiness leads to growth and
enlightenment, both of which are steps on
the ladder toward transcending grief.

. . . .

Happy women know that no one gets
to be happy all the time.

. . . .

Happy women know that a good attitude,
valued relationships, and a meaningful life are
the central ingredients for happiness.

. . . .

Bibliography

Bianchi, Suzanne M., John P. Robinson, and Melissa A. Milkie. *Changing Rhythms of American Family Life*. New York: Russell Sage Foundation, 2006.

Bly, Robert. *The Sibling Society*. New York: Random House Value Publishing, 1998.

Braiker, Harriet. *The Disease to Please*. New York: McGraw Hill, 2000.

Brizendine, Louann. *The Female Brain*. New York: Morgan Road, 2006.

Clarke, Edward. *Sex in Education*. Manchester, NH: Ayer, 1972.

Crowley, Chris, and Henry Lodge. *Younger Next Year for Women*. New York: Workman, 2005.

Frankl, Viktor E. *Man's Search for Meaning*. Boston: Beacon Press, 2006.

Friedan, Betty. *The Feminine Mystique*. New York: W. W. Norton, 1963.

Fuller, Bonnie. *The Joys of Much Too Much*. New York: Fireside, 2006.

Gilbert, Daniel. *Stumbling on Happiness*. New York: Knopf, 2006.

Goleman, Daniel. *Emotional Intelligence*. New York: Bantam, 2006.

Kasser, Tim. *The High Price of Materialism*. Cambridge, MA: MIT Press, 2002.

Kushner, Harold. *When Bad Things Happen to Good People*. New York: Schocken, 2001.

Levenkron, Steven. *The Best Little Girl in the World*. New York: Warner, 1978

Luskin, Frederic. *Forgive for Good*. San Francisco: HarperSanFrancisco, 2001.

Meili, Trisha. *I Am the Central Park Jogger*. New York: Scribner's, 2003.

Morris, Tom. *If Aristotle Ran General Motors*. New York: Henry Holt, 1997.

Nettle, Daniel. *Happiness*. New York: Oxford University Press USA, 2005.

Tiger, Lionel. *Optimism*. New York: Simon & Schuster, 1979.

Wolf, Naomi. *The Beauty Myth. New York: Harper Perennial, 2002.*

Index

Underscored page references indicate boxed text.

A

Abandonment fear, as reason for people pleasing, 65

ABC principle, influencing attitude, 126

Abortion, legalization of, 137

Abused women
case study on, 116 19, 123
escape attempts of, 6
fear of abandonment in, 65
as pleasers, 64
reasons for remaining, 119–21

Achievement, self-esteem from, 33

Activities, multiple, of centenarians, 158

Adaptivity vs. learned helplessness, 11

Adler, Alfred, 9

Advertising
promises of happiness in, 50
"real models" in, 29

Affluence
burdens of
case study on, 56–57
increased choices, 57–58
inflated expectations, 54–55
too much of a good thing, 56–57
myths of, 44–45
happiness is infinite, 52–54
money buys happiness, 48–51
money buys security, 45–48
unrelated to happiness, 13, 58–60

Age discrimination, careers and, 147

Aggression, male vs. female brain and, xiii

Aging
benefits of positive perception of, 32–33
perfectionism and, 30–32
vanity issues and, 147–48

Alice syndrome, 176

Altruism, 84, 170
as quality of happy women, 213–16

Amygdala, 99–101, 122, 123, 178

Anger
arteriosclerosis and, 181
fear of, as reason for people pleasing, 67–68
as major emotion, 13
as resolvable emotion, 3
suppressed, effects of, 88–89
as survival emotion, 17
unresolved, 97–99

Anorexia, 29–30

Apathy, 3

Apologies, as perfectionist tendency, 21

Appreciation
for freedom from money trap, 60–61
of life, as quality of happy women, 220–22
in positive psychology, 5, 8
power of, 169–70

Arrogance, from comparison to others, 51

239

Arteriosclerosis, emotions increasing
risk of, 181
Attitude, influencing happiness, 125–26
Attractiveness, importance of, as
contributor to perfectionism,
27–28

B

Bayer, Alan, 39–40
Balance
between career and personal life,
151–53
finding, 78
Bauer, Jack, 159
Bauman, Leslie, 152
Beauty
finding, amid adversity, 172–73
in positive psychology, 6
Beauty industry, encouraging
perfectionism, 28–29
Belief in higher power, for transcending
grief, 171–72
Belief in oneself, as quality of happy
women, 201–4
Bennett, Neil, 142
Bereavement. *See* Loss
Berry, Julia, 218–20, 229–30
Best Little Girl in the World, The, 30
Bianchi, Suzanne, 146
Birth control pill, women's movement
and, 136, 137
Blame
as disempowering, 95
revenge and, 96
Blanchflower, David, 54
Bloom, David, 142
Bly, Robert, 154
Bobbitt, Lorena, 89
Body, taking care of, 75–76

Boham, Elizabeth, 165–66
Boundaries, vs. respect, 85
Braiker, Harriet, 63
Brain
emotional memories stored in,
99–100
evolution of, 15–16, 121–22
gender differences in, xii–xiii
mammalian or limbic, 16, 122, 178
meditation affecting, 197, 198
mirror neurons in, 192–93
neocortex, 16–17, 121, 122, 123, 178
reptilian, 16, 121–22, 178
Brewer, Lynn, 209, 211–13, 218, 230
Brickman, Philip, 52
Brizendine, Louann, xiii, 182
Broaden and build theory, 127
Buffet, Warren, 147
Bulik, Cynthia, 29
Bulimia, 29
Buttafuocco, Joey, 89

C

Cacciatore, Joanne, 162, 171, 209, 214–
16, 220, 230
Calling, definition of, 133
Campbell, Donald, 52
Campbell, W. Keith, 109
Career(s). *See also* Career traps
avoiding overwork in, 150–51
balancing, with personal life, 151–53
benefits of, 133–34
definition of, 133
overcommitment to, xvii–xviii
of women
television portrayal of, 135–36
Women's Movement and, 136–39
women's stories about, 202–4, 206–8,
211

E

F

Q

R

S

W

Wanton wanting, xvi–xvii. *See also* Affluence

Welch, Jack, 147

Westphal, Jenifer, 201–2, 223, 224, 232

What Happy People Know, xii

When Bad Things Happen to Good People, 155

Whittlesey, Faith, 139

Williams, Jesse, 176

Winning attitude, in overcoming perfectionism, 41–42

Wisdom, as quality of happy women, 223–25

Wolf, Naomi, 28

Women
    brain of, xii, xiii
    as caretakers, 82–83
    fear in, 17
    fearing relationship breakups, 110–11
    hormonal effects on, 182–83, 184–85
    men as necessity for, 111–12
    as people pleasers, 63, 64
        fears contributing to, 64–68
    perfectionism in, 24
    as relationship centered, xiii, xiv, 17, 63–64, 65, 190
    revenge ruts in, 88, 89
    television portrayal of, 135–36

Women's Movement, 136–39
    timeline of, 137

Work, categories of, 133

Wuornos, Aileen, 89

Y

Younger Next Year for Women, 191

Youth, obsession with, as contributor to perfectionism, 30–33

About the Authors

Dan Baker, PhD

While his educational training was soundly grounded in traditional counseling psychology, Dan's desire to understand more about human-beings "work" took him into the study of medical psychology. Throughout his training he questioned the intense and almost exclusive focus on problems and pathology. Understanding that the mere absence of disease no more meant robust health than curing depression meant that one then got to be happy. He began to ponder what would happen if he turned his attention to the study of values, character, and the strengths of humanity? What was discovered first was that we find what we seek: Go looking for problems and they will be found. Go looking for resilience, noble character, and happiness and the universe will yield little by little the factors and dynamics that lead to the good life. He has been the benefactor of learning from the many women—some who were happy and many who struggled with life—who have sought his counsel over the past 30 years.

Cathy Greenberg, PhD

Cathy's professional start began in the natural world of primates. True to the tradition of many scientists in this field, she started to raise questions regarding the applicability of what she was learning to human beings and their organizations. In time there was a natural transition from the arboreal domain to the corporate boardroom. She has now accumulated more than two decades of high-level experience, which has lead to innumerable opportunities to better people and organizations. Her orientation has always been toward constructive interaction, which yields positive outcomes. Not only a student of leadership, she is also a practitioner by virtue of holding high-ranking positions as a founding partner in CSC's Global Organizational Change Practice and managing partner in the Accenture Institute for Strategic Change. During her career she has coached women from all walks of life, consequently gleaning invaluable knowledge of what happy women know.

Ina Yalof

Ina is a writer with a background as a medical sociologist. She is the author or coauthor of 11 books. She teaches writing for Dartmouth College's Institute for Lifelong Education at Dartmouth (ILEAD) program.